1 Sauce, 100 Recipes

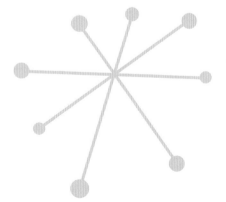

1 Sauce, 100 Recipes

Linda Doeser

First published in 2010
LOVE FOOD is an imprint of Parragon Books Ltd

Parragon
Queen Street House
4 Queen Street
Bath BA1 1HE, UK

Copyright © Parragon Books Ltd 2010

ISBN: 978-1-4075-5376-4

Printed in China

Written by Linda Doeser
Photography by Mike Cooper
Home economy by Lincoln Jefferson

Notes for the Reader
This book uses imperial, metric, and US cup measurements. Follow
the same units of measurement throughout; do not mix imperial and
metric. All spoon measurements are level: teaspoons are assumed to
be 5 ml, and tablespoons are assumed to be 15 ml. Unless otherwise
stated, milk is assumed to be whole, individual vegetables are
medium, eggs are large, and pepper is freshly ground black pepper.

The times given are an approximate guide only. Preparation times
differ according to the techniques used by different people and the
cooking times may also vary from those given as a result of the type
of oven used. Optional ingredients, variations, or serving suggestions
have not been included in the calculations.

Recipes using raw or very lightly cooked eggs should be avoided
by infants, the elderly, pregnant women, convalescents, and anyone
with a chronic condition. Pregnant and breast-feeding women are
advised to avoid eating peanuts and peanut products. People with
nut allergies should be aware that some of the prepared ingredients
used in the recipes in this book may contain nuts. Always check the
package before use.

Picture Acknowledgment
Front cover image: Lasagne with minced beef © Louise Lister/
StockFood Creative/Getty Images

Contents

Introduction

A well-made, tasty sauce is often the secret that turns a good dish into a great one—and there are few sauces that are more versatile and more popular than tomato sauce. It makes a great accompaniment to plainly cooked meat, poultry, fish, vegetables, and eggs, and works superbly well as the basis for braised dishes, stews, and baked layered dishes. It's the perfect topping for pasta, essential for classic pizzas, and makes a delicious hot or cold dipping sauce for all kinds of vegetables and fritters.

A simple tomato sauce is quick and easy to make. There's no risk of curdling and it doesn't require much attention while it simmers. It can be made in advance and reheated, the ingredients are inexpensive and readily available, and it keeps well in the refrigerator and freezer. All the dishes in this book can be made with just the basic sauce—and will be truly delicious—but the recipes also include a huge number of variations. Tomatoes go so well with other ingredients—from chiles to mushrooms and from almonds to olives—that the options are almost endless. There are substantial versions that include bacon, cheese, corn, beans, or other vegetables; spicy sauces with warm Middle Eastern flavors, hot Mexican chiles, subtle Indian mixes, or a savory barbecue tang; rich sauces with cream, butter, yogurt, wine, or sherry; and piquant mixtures with olives, capers, oranges, horseradish, anchovies, or apples.

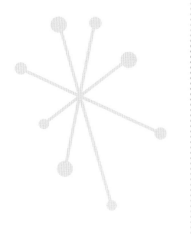

Basic Tomato Sauce Ingredients

Tomatoes are, of course, the main and most important ingredient and there is debate about whether fresh or canned tomatoes make the best sauce. Fresh tomatoes that have ripened fully in the sun are sweet and full of flavor—particularly if they're homegrown—and will almost certainly make a really tasty sauce. However, out-of-season tomatoes that have to be imported may have been picked before they are ripe and are often watery and tasteless. Good-quality canned tomatoes are available all year round and are excellent for making tomato sauce. In blind tastings, many people have either been unable to taste any difference between the same sauce made with fresh and canned tomatoes or have actually preferred the one made with canned.

Plum tomatoes, whether fresh or canned, are perfect for cooking because they have denser, less watery flesh than round tomatoes. Many round tomato varieties are selected by suppliers because they are robust enough to withstand the rigors of transportation rather than for their flavor, although recent years have seen an increase in the range of tomatoes available. Cherry tomatoes tend to be more expensive but are usually sweet and fragrant. Never use unripe tomatoes for making tomato sauce as no amount of added sugar will counteract their acidity and sharpness—keep them for making chutney. However, you can use varieties that turn yellow when ripe, but the sauce may be less visually appealing than when made with red tomatoes.

Tomato paste intensifies the flavor of tomatoes and is particularly useful if you are using fresh tomatoes that may not have been sun-ripened. Sugar helps to counteract the acidity of tomatoes, some of which can be very sharp. A useful tip when you don't have any tomato paste is to omit the sugar and add 1–2 tablespoons of ketchup instead.

Various members of the onion family add flavor and emphasis to tomato sauce. The common yellow onion is a good all-rounder and can be used in any recipe but some recipes work even better with other varieties. Sweet onions include red onions, which have reddish-purple skins and pink-tinged flesh, and Bermuda onions, which are very large and mild with a mellow flavor. Shallots are much smaller than most varieties of onion and are elongated in shape. They are far less astringent than onions, although they do vary in strength and have a distinctive taste that is not quite onion and not quite garlic. Scallions, with a white bulb and leafy green tops, are mild and cook quickly. Garlic is a natural partner for tomatoes and gives extra depth to the flavor of the sauce. The number of cloves to include is a matter of personal taste. If you are not very keen on the flavor, add a whole clove when softening the onion and then remove and discard it before adding the other ingredients. This will give just a hint of garlic that you won't find overwhelming.

Most recipes in this book recommend using olive oil, which not only has a rich flavor and aroma that complement tomatoes but is also a healthy choice as it contains monounsaturated fat. It just seems to go perfectly with the flavor of tomatoes and is the natural choice for Mediterranean and Middle Eastern recipes. You do not need to use expensive extra virgin oil—keep that for salad dressings. Virgin oil, from the second pressing is perfect for cooking, but avoid olive oils simply labeled "pure" because they may have been heat-treated and consequently have lost all flavor. If you're using other vegetable oils, perhaps because the sauce is very spicy, choose one with a bland flavor, such as sunflower, safflower, peanut, or corn oil.

As a rule, fresh herbs are always more flavorsome than dried, although both bay leaves and oregano are often used dried. Basil is the tomato herb as it complements the flavor superbly. The leaves

are easily bruised so it is often better to tear them by hand rather than to chop them with a knife. Both curly and flat-leaf parsley and fresh cilantro are also good choices. One or two bay leaves add a distinctive flavor and aroma to robust tomato sauces but don't forget to remove them before serving.

The final ingredient in the basic tomato sauce is celery, which provides extra flavor and texture. If you don't like the "strings" in celery, they can be removed easily by running a vegetable peeler along the length of the stalk.

Preparing Fresh Tomatoes

To peel tomatoes, cut a cross in the top of the tomatoes and put them into a heatproof bowl. Pour in boiling water to cover and let stand for 1 minute. Drain and peel off the skins with a sharp knife; they should slip off easily. Don't try to peel more than 4–5 tomatoes at a time or some will begin to cook in the boiling water.

If you have a gas stove, you can also peel tomatoes by skewering them, 1 at a time, with a metal fork, holding them in the gas flame, and turning for 1–2 minutes, until the skin splits and wrinkles. Let cool, then pull off the skins with your fingers.

Always cut out the top part of the tomato where the stem grew and the central pale core, which is hard and inedible, using a sharp knife.

Most recipes in this book do not suggest seeding tomatoes, but a few do. There are also recipes where the finished sauce should be pressed through a strainer. This removes the seeds as well as the vegetables and other solid matter.

To seed tomatoes, cut them in half with a sharp knife, then scoop out the seeds using a teaspoon.

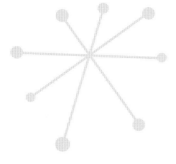

Basic Tomato Sauce

Makes about 2½ cups

* ☀ 2 tbsp butter
* ☀ 2 tbsp olive or other vegetable oil
* ☀ 1 onion, finely chopped
* ☀ 1 garlic clove, finely chopped
* ☀ 1 celery stalk, finely chopped
* ☀ 400 g/14 oz canned chopped tomatoes or 500 g/
   1 lb 2 oz plum tomatoes, peeled, cored, and chopped
* ☀ 2 tbsp tomato paste
* ☀ brown sugar, to taste
* ☀ 1–2 tbsp chopped fresh herbs and/or 1–2 tsp dried
   herbs, and/or 1–2 bay leaves
* ☀ scant ½ cup water
* ☀ salt and pepper

Melt the butter with the oil in a pan. Add the onion, garlic, and celery and cook over low heat, stirring occasionally, for 5 minutes, until softened. Stir in the tomatoes, tomato paste, sugar to taste, herbs, and water and season to taste with salt and pepper. Increase the heat to medium and bring to a boil, then reduce the heat and simmer, stirring occasionally, for 15–20 minutes, until thickened.

This is the basic recipe that all 100 dishes in this book are based on. For each recipe, the ingredients are highlighted (☀) for easy reference. Please note that quantities may vary so please check these carefully.

Easy

Barbecued Beef Kabobs

1. First, make the sauce. Melt the butter with the oil in a pan. Add the onion, garlic, and celery and cook over low heat, stirring occasionally, for 5 minutes, until softened. Add the chiles and cook, stirring occasionally, for an additional 3 minutes. Stir in the tomatoes, tomato paste, mustard powder, bay leaf, Worcestershire sauce, honey, and vinegar and season to taste with salt and pepper. Increase the heat to medium and bring to a boil, then reduce the heat and simmer, stirring occasionally, for 15–20 minutes, until thickened.

2. Remove the pan from the heat and let cool slightly. Remove and discard the bay leaf, transfer the sauce to a food processor, and process until smooth. Press the sauce through a strainer into a bowl.

3. Preheat the barbecue or broiler. Brush 4 metal skewers with oil. Cut each red onion into 8 wedges. Trim the scallions and cut in half widthwise. Thread the steak cubes onto the skewers, alternating them with the onion wedges and scallion halves.

4. Transfer about three-quarters of the barbecue sauce to a sauceboat. Brush half the remainder over the kabobs and cook on the barbecue or under the broiler for 8–10 minutes, turning frequently and brushing with the remaining sauce from the bowl, until the meat is cooked to your liking. Serve immediately with the reserved sauce.

Serves 4

olive oil, for brushing

2 red onions

4 scallions

1 lb 9 oz/700 g sirloin steak, cut into cubes

Barbecue sauce

* 2 tbsp butter
* 2 tbsp olive oil

1 Bermuda onion, finely chopped

* 2 garlic cloves, finely chopped
* 1 celery stalk, finely chopped

1–2 fresh red chiles, seeded and chopped

* 14 oz/400 g canned chopped tomatoes
* 2 tbsp tomato paste

1 tsp mustard powder

* 1 bay leaf

2 tbsp Worcestershire sauce

3 tbsp honey

1 tbsp red wine vinegar

* salt and pepper

Minestrone

1. Cook the bacon in a large pan over low heat, stirring occasionally, for 2–3 minutes, until the fat runs. Add the potatoes, carrot, celery, and zucchini and cook, stirring occasionally, for 10 minutes.

2. Pour the tomato sauce into the pan with the vegetables, then stir in the stock and add the cannellini beans, parsley, sage, and basil. Increase the heat to medium and bring to a boil, then reduce the heat and simmer for 5 minutes.

3. Add the peas and pasta, bring back to a boil, and simmer for an additional 10 minutes. Taste and adjust the seasoning, adding salt and pepper if needed. Ladle into warmed bowls and serve immediately.

Serves 4

2 slices bacon, chopped

2 potatoes, diced

1 carrot, sliced

1 celery stalk, sliced

1 zucchini, sliced

1 quantity Basic Tomato Sauce (see page 10)

3¾ cups chicken or vegetable stock

14 oz/400 g canned cannellini beans, drained and rinsed

1 tbsp chopped fresh flat-leaf parsley

1 fresh sage sprig, chopped

1 fresh basil sprig, chopped

1 cup frozen peas

½ cup dried farfallini (small bow tie pasta)

salt and pepper

White Beans with Prosciutto & Tomato Sauce

1. Put the beans into a large pan, pour in water to cover, and bring to a boil over medium–high heat. Reduce the heat and simmer for 45 minutes, until the beans are just tender. Drain well.

2. Melt the butter with the oil in a pan. Add the onions, garlic, and celery and cook over low heat, stirring occasionally, for 5 minutes, until softened. Stir in the tomatoes, tomato paste, sugar to taste, basil, prosciutto, and water and season to taste with salt and pepper. Increase the heat to medium and bring to a boil.

3. Add the beans, reduce the heat, and simmer, stirring occasionally, for 30 minutes. Transfer to a warmed serving dish and serve immediately.

Serves 4–6

- 2¾ cups dried navy beans, soaked overnight and drained
- 4 tbsp butter
- 4 tbsp olive oil
- 2 onions, finely chopped
- 2 garlic cloves, finely chopped
- 2 celery stalks, finely chopped
- 1 lb 12 oz/800 g canned chopped tomatoes
- 2 tbsp tomato paste
- brown sugar, to taste
- 1 tbsp chopped fresh basil
- ⅔ cup chopped prosciutto
- scant ½ cup water
- salt and pepper

Ham Italian Style

1. First, make the sauce. Melt the butter with the oil in a pan. Add the shallots, garlic, and celery and cook over low heat, stirring occasionally, for 5 minutes, until softened. Stir in the tomatoes, tomato paste, sugar to taste, parsley, and wine and season to taste with salt and pepper. Increase the heat to medium and bring to a boil, then reduce the heat and simmer, stirring occasionally, for 15–20 minutes, until thickened.

2. Meanwhile, preheat the broiler. Bring a large pan of lightly salted water to a boil. Add the pasta, bring back to a boil, and cook for 8–10 minutes, until tender but still firm to the bite. Rub the ham steaks with the sage and cook under the preheated broiler for 6–7 minutes on each side, until tender and cooked through.

3. Drain the pasta, put into a warmed serving dish, and toss with the butter. Put the ham steaks on top and pour the tomato sauce over them. Sprinkle with the olives and serve immediately.

Serves 4

8 oz/225 g dried tagliatelle verde

4 thick ham steaks

1 tsp dried sage

2 tbsp butter

8 black olives, pitted and halved

salt

Tomato sauce

2 tbsp butter

2 tbsp olive oil

2 shallots, finely chopped

2 garlic cloves, finely chopped

1 celery stalk, finely chopped

14 oz/400 g canned chopped tomatoes

2 tbsp tomato paste

brown sugar, to taste

1 tbsp chopped fresh flat-leaf parsley

scant ½ cup dry white wine

salt and pepper

Ham & Asparagus Rolls in Sun-Dried Tomato Sauce

1. First, make the sauce. Melt the butter with the oil in a pan. Add the shallots and celery and cook over low heat, stirring occasionally, for 5 minutes, until softened. Stir in the fresh and sun-dried tomatoes, sun-dried tomato paste, sugar to taste, basil, olives, and water and season to taste with salt and pepper. Increase the heat to medium and bring to a boil, then reduce the heat and simmer, stirring occasionally, for 15–20 minutes, until thickened.

2. Meanwhile, preheat the oven to 350°C/180°C. Divide the asparagus spears equally among the slices of ham. Roll up the ham and put the rolls, seam-side down, into a large ovenproof dish.

3. Pour the sauce over the ham rolls, sprinkle with the Parmesan, and bake in the preheated oven for 20 minutes. Serve immediately.

Serves 6

1 lb 14 oz/850 g canned asparagus spears, drained
12 slices cooked ham
⅔ cup grated Parmesan cheese

Sun-dried tomato sauce
* 2 tbsp butter
* 2 tbsp olive oil
2 shallots, finely chopped
* 1 celery stalk, finely chopped
* 1 lb 2 oz/500 g plum tomatoes, peeled, cored, and chopped
12 sun-dried tomatoes in oil, drained and chopped
2 tbsp sun-dried tomato paste
* brown sugar, to taste
* 1 tbsp chopped fresh basil
½ cup sliced pitted black olives
* scant ½ cup water
* salt and pepper

Pork Chops with Tomato & Olive Sauce

1. Rub the chops all over with salt, pepper, and the oregano. Melt 4 tablespoons of the butter with the oil in a large sauté pan or skillet. Add the onion, garlic, and celery and cook over low heat, stirring occasionally, for 5 minutes, until softened. Add the chops in a single layer, increase the heat to medium, and cook for 3–5 minutes on each side, until lightly browned.

2. Add the tomatoes, tomato paste, sugar, and wine and season to taste with salt and pepper. Bring to a boil, then reduce the heat, cover, and simmer for 15 minutes. Add the olives, re-cover the pan, and simmer for an additional 5–10 minutes, until the chops are tender and cooked through.

3. Meanwhile, put the remaining butter and the flour on a saucer and work together with your fingertips until a smooth paste (beurre manié) forms. Shape into several small balls.

4. Transfer the chops to a warmed serving plate and keep warm. Add the beurre manié to the sauce, 1 piece at a time, stirring constantly. Make sure each piece has been fully incorporated before adding the next. Cook, stirring constantly, for 2–3 minutes. Pour the sauce over the chops, garnish with parsley, and serve immediately.

Serves 6

6 pork chops

1 tsp dried oregano

* 5 tbsp butter

* 4 tbsp olive oil

* 1 large onion, finely chopped

* 2 garlic cloves, finely chopped

* 1 celery stalk, finely chopped

* 14 oz/400 g canned chopped tomatoes

* 2 tbsp tomato paste

* 1 tsp brown sugar, or to taste

½ cup red wine

½ cup chopped pimiento-stuffed olives

2 tbsp all-purpose flour

* salt and pepper

chopped fresh flat-leaf parsley, to garnish

Lamb in Tomato Sauce

1. Melt the butter in a large pan. Add the lamb and cook over medium heat, stirring frequently, for 6–8 minutes, until evenly browned. Stir in the garlic, ½ cup of the wine, and the stock, season to taste with salt and pepper, and bring to a boil. Reduce the heat and simmer, stirring occasionally, for 30 minutes, until the lamb is tender.

2. Meanwhile, make the sauce. Melt the butter with the oil in a pan. Add the shallots, garlic, and celery and cook over low heat, stirring occasionally, for 5 minutes, until softened. Stir in the tomatoes, tomato paste, sugar to taste, parsley, and water and season to taste with salt and pepper. Increase the heat to medium and bring to a boil, then reduce the heat and simmer, stirring occasionally, for 15–20 minutes, until thickened.

3. Mix the flour to a paste with the remaining wine in a small bowl, then stir into the lamb mixture. Cook, stirring constantly, for 3 minutes, or until the cooking liquid has thickened. Stir in the sauce.

4. Transfer the stew to a warmed serving dish, garnish with parsley, and serve immediately.

Serves 4

4 tbsp butter

2 lb 4 oz/1 kg boned shoulder of lamb, trimmed and cut into 1½-inch/4-cm cubes

1 garlic clove, finely chopped

⅔ cup dry white wine

1 cup chicken stock

1 tbsp all-purpose flour

salt and pepper

Tomato sauce

2 tbsp butter

2 tbsp olive oil

2 shallots, finely chopped

2 garlic cloves, finely chopped

1 celery stalk, finely chopped

14 oz/400 g canned chopped tomatoes

2 tbsp tomato paste

brown sugar, to taste

2 tbsp chopped fresh flat-leaf parsley, plus extra to garnish

scant ½ cup water

salt and pepper

Chicken Croquettes in Rich Tomato Sauce

1. Heat half the oil in a large pan. Add the onion and celery and cook over low heat, stirring occasionally, for 5 minutes, until softened. Add the chicken, tomatoes, and potatoes and cook, stirring frequently, for 8–10 minutes. Transfer to a food processor and process until smooth. Scrape into a bowl and let cool, then chill for 1 hour.

2. Meanwhile, make the sauce. Remove the bacon rind and dice the bacon. Melt the butter with the bacon rind in a pan. Add the bacon, shallot, garlic, celery, and carrot and cook over low heat, stirring occasionally, for 5 minutes. Stir in the tomatoes and cook, stirring occasionally, for 5 minutes. Stir the cornstarch into the stock and pour it into the pan. Season to taste with salt and pepper. Cover and simmer, stirring occasionally, for 20 minutes, until thickened. Remove and discard the bacon rind.

3. Lightly dust your hands with flour and divide the chicken mixture into 8–12 pieces. Roll each into a small croquette. Place the eggs in a shallow bowl and spread out the breadcrumbs in a separate shallow bowl. Dip the croquettes into the beaten egg, then into the breadcrumbs to coat.

4. Heat the remaining oil in a skillet. Add the croquettes and cook over medium heat, turning once, for 10 minutes. Drain on paper towels. Pour the sauce over the croquettes, sprinkle with the parsley, and serve immediately.

Serves 4

6 tbsp olive oil

1 onion, finely chopped

1 celery stalk, finely chopped

1⅔ cups finely chopped cooked chicken

3 tomatoes, peeled and finely chopped

4 boiled potatoes, finely chopped

all-purpose flour, for dusting

2 eggs, lightly beaten

1⅔ cups dry breadcrumbs

1 tbsp chopped fresh parsley

Rich tomato sauce

1 slice lean bacon

2 tbsp butter

1 shallot, finely chopped

1 garlic clove, finely chopped

1 celery stalk, finely chopped

1 carrot, finely chopped

14 oz/400 g canned chopped tomatoes

2 tsp cornstarch

1¼ cups chicken stock

salt and pepper

Chicken & Eggplant Layers Baked in Tomato Sauce

1. Put the chicken between 2 sheets of plastic wrap and beat until thin and even. Cut into 4-inch/10-cm pieces and set aside.

2. To make the sauce, melt the butter with the oil in a pan. Add the onion, garlic, and celery and cook over low heat, stirring occasionally, for 5 minutes, until softened. Stir in the tomatoes, tomato paste, olives, sugar to taste, oregano, and water and season to taste with salt and pepper. Increase the heat to medium and bring to a boil, then reduce the heat and simmer, stirring occasionally, for 15–20 minutes, until thickened.

3. Meanwhile, dip the eggplant slices in the flour to coat. Heat 5 tablespoons of the oil in a large skillet and cook the eggplant slices, in batches, for 3 minutes on each side, until lightly browned, adding more oil as necessary.

4. Preheat the oven to 350°F/180°C. Spread out the breadcrumbs in a shallow dish and lightly beat the egg in a separate shallow dish. Dip the chicken first in the egg and then in the breadcrumbs to coat. Heat the remaining oil in the skillet. Add the chicken and cook over medium heat for 2 minutes on each side, until golden.

5. Layer the chicken and eggplant slices in an ovenproof dish, pour over the sauce, and sprinkle with the Parmesan. Bake in the preheated oven for 20 minutes, until golden. Garnish with parsley and serve immediately.

Serves 4

4 skinless, boneless chicken breasts, about 6 oz/175 g each

2 eggplants, sliced

4 tbsp all-purpose flour

generous 1 cup olive oil

scant 1 cup dry breadcrumbs

1 egg

⅔ cup grated Parmesan cheese

chopped fresh flat-leaf parsley, to garnish

Tomato sauce

- 2 tbsp butter
- 2 tbsp olive oil
- 1 onion, finely chopped
- 2 garlic cloves, finely chopped
- 1 celery stalk, finely chopped
- 14 oz/400 g canned chopped tomatoes
- 2 tbsp tomato paste
- 6 pitted olives, sliced
- brown sugar, to taste
- 1 tsp dried oregano
- scant ½ cup water
- salt and pepper

Pasta with Tomato & Anchovy Sauce

1. First, make the sauce. Melt the butter with the oil in a pan. Add the shallots, garlic, and celery and cook over low heat, stirring occasionally, for 5 minutes, until softened. Stir in the tomatoes, tomato paste, sugar to taste, parsley, oregano, anchovies, and water and season to taste with pepper. Increase the heat to medium and bring to a boil, then reduce the heat and simmer, stirring occasionally, for 30 minutes, until thickened.

2. Meanwhile, bring a large pan of lightly salted water to a boil. Add the spaghetti, bring back to a boil, and cook for 8–10 minutes, until tender but still firm to the bite. Drain and put into a warmed serving dish.

3. Taste the sauce and adjust the seasoning, adding salt and pepper if needed. Pour the sauce over the pasta and toss well. Garnish with parsley and serve immediately.

Serves 4

1 lb/450 g dried spaghetti
salt

Tomato & anchovy sauce
* 2 tbsp butter
* 2 tbsp olive oil
2 shallots, finely chopped
* 2 garlic cloves, finely chopped
* 1 celery stalk, finely chopped
* 14 oz/400 g canned chopped tomatoes
* 2 tbsp tomato paste
* brown sugar, to taste
* 1 tbsp chopped fresh flat-leaf parsley, plus extra to garnish
* pinch of dried oregano
8 canned anchovy fillets, drained and chopped
* scant ½ cup water
* salt and pepper

Baked Trout in Tomato Sauce

1. First, make the sauce. Melt the butter with the oil in a pan. Add the onion, garlic, and celery and cook over low heat, stirring occasionally, for 5 minutes, until softened. Stir in the tomatoes, tomato paste, sugar to taste, and water and season to taste with salt and pepper. Increase the heat to medium and bring to a boil, then reduce the heat and simmer, stirring occasionally, for 15–20 minutes, until thickened.

2. Meanwhile, preheat the oven to 350°F/180°C. Spread out the flour in a shallow dish and season to taste with salt and pepper. Add the trout, 1 at a time, and turn to coat well in the flour, then shake off any excess.

3. Heat the oil in a flameproof casserole. Add the fish and cook over medium heat for 3–4 minutes on each side, until lightly browned. Pour the sauce over the fish, cover, and bake in the preheated oven for 10–15 minutes, until the flesh flakes easily. Sprinkle with the parsley and serve immediately.

Serves 4

½ cup all-purpose flour
4 trout, cleaned
3 tbsp olive oil
1 tbsp chopped fresh parsley
salt and pepper

Tomato sauce
* 2 tbsp butter
* 2 tbsp olive oil
* 1 onion, finely chopped
* 3 garlic cloves, finely chopped
* 2 celery stalks, finely chopped
* 2 lb 4 oz/1 kg plum tomatoes, peeled, cored, and chopped
* 4 tbsp tomato paste
* brown sugar, to taste
* scant ½ cup water
* salt and pepper

Sole with Tomato Sauce

1. First, make the sauce. Melt the butter with the oil in a pan. Add the onion, garlic, and celery and cook over low heat, stirring occasionally, for 5 minutes, until softened. Stir in the tomatoes, tomato paste, sugar to taste, parsley, and water and season to taste with salt and pepper. Increase the heat to medium and bring to a boil, then reduce the heat and simmer, stirring occasionally, for 20 minutes, until thickened.

2. Meanwhile, preheat the oven to 350°F/180°C. Trim the sides of the fish fillets to make them straight, reserving the trimmings, then cut them in half lengthwise. Season to taste with salt and pepper and sprinkle with the lemon juice.

3. Lightly beat the ricotta in a bowl with a fork until smooth. Chop the fish trimmings and stir them into the ricotta with the Tabasco. Spread the mixture over the strips of fish and roll up. Put the rolls into an ovenproof dish, seam-side down, in a single layer. Pour the stock over them and bake in the preheated oven for 20 minutes, until the fish flakes easily.

4. Using a slotted spoon, carefully transfer the fish rolls to a warmed serving dish. Spoon the tomato sauce over them and sprinkle over the olives and dill pickle. Serve immediately.

Serves 4

4 large sole fillets, skinned

2 tbsp lemon juice

¼ cup ricotta cheese

dash of Tabasco sauce

1¼ cups fish stock

4 black olives, pitted and halved

1 dill pickle, chopped

salt and pepper

Tomato sauce

※ 2 tbsp butter

※ 2 tbsp olive oil

※ 1 onion, finely chopped

※ 2 garlic cloves, finely chopped

※ 1 celery stalk, finely chopped

※ 14 oz/400 g canned chopped tomatoes

※ 2 tbsp tomato paste

※ brown sugar, to taste

※ 1 tbsp chopped fresh flat-leaf parsley

※ scant ½ cup water

※ salt and pepper

Breaded Swordfish with Tomato & Zucchini Sauce

1. First, make the sauce. Melt the butter with the oil in a large pan. Add the onion, garlic, celery, and zucchini and cook over low heat, stirring occasionally, for 8–10 minutes, until lightly browned. Stir in the tomatoes, tomato paste, capers, cayenne pepper, and water and season to taste with salt and pepper. Increase the heat to medium and bring to a boil, then reduce the heat and simmer, stirring occasionally, for 15 minutes, until thickened.

2. Meanwhile, cut the fish steaks in half. Combine the breadcrumbs and oregano in a shallow dish and lightly beat the eggs in a separate shallow dish. Dip the pieces of swordfish first into the eggs and then into the breadcrumb mixture to coat.

3. Melt the butter in a large skillet. Add the pieces of fish and cook over medium heat, turning occasionally, for 6–8 minutes, until lightly browned.

4. Transfer the pieces of fish to the pan and spoon the sauce over them. Simmer gently, stirring occasionally, for an additional 15 minutes, until the fish flakes easily. Transfer to a warmed serving dish and serve immediately.

Serves 4

4 swordfish steaks, about 8 oz/225 g each
1¼ cups dry breadcrumbs
1 tsp dried oregano
2 eggs
4 tbsp butter

Tomato & zucchini sauce
2 tbsp butter
2 tbsp olive oil
1 Bermuda onion, finely chopped
2 garlic cloves, finely chopped
1 celery stalk, finely chopped
3 zucchini, cut into ¼-inch/ 5-mm slices
14 oz/400 g canned chopped tomatoes
2 tbsp tomato paste
1 tbsp drained capers
pinch of cayenne pepper
scant ½ cup water
salt and pepper

Shrimp & Feta in Tomato Sauce

1. First, make the sauce. Melt the butter with the oil in a pan. Add the onion, garlic, and celery and cook over low heat, stirring occasionally, for 5 minutes, until softened. Stir in the tomatoes, tomato paste, sugar to taste, herbs, and water. Increase the heat to medium and bring to a boil, then reduce the heat and simmer, stirring occasionally, for 15 minutes.

2. Stir in the wine and season to taste with salt and pepper. Increase the heat and bring to a boil, then reduce the heat and simmer, stirring occasionally, for an additional 30 minutes, until thickened.

3. Stir in the shrimp and feta cheese and cook, stirring frequently, for 5–8 minutes, until the shrimp have turned pink and the cheese has melted. Remove and discard the bay leaf. Transfer to a warmed serving dish and serve immediately.

Serves 4

1 lb 2 oz/500 g jumbo shrimp, peeled and deveined
¾ cup crumbled feta cheese

Tomato sauce
* 2 tbsp butter
* 2 tbsp olive oil
* 1 onion, finely chopped
* 3 garlic cloves, finely chopped
* 1 celery stalk, finely chopped
* 2 lb 4 oz/1 kg plum tomatoes, peeled, cored and chopped
* 2 tbsp tomato paste
* brown sugar, to taste
* 1 tbsp chopped fresh flat-leaf parsley
* 1 fresh basil sprig, chopped
* 1 bay leaf
* ½ tsp dried oregano
* scant ½ cup water
* 1 cup dry white wine
* salt and pepper

Succulent Tomato Shellfish

1. First, make the sauce. Melt the butter with the oil in a large pan. Add the shallot, garlic, and celery and cook over low heat, stirring occasionally, for 5 minutes, until softened. Stir in the tomatoes, tomato paste, sugar to taste, parsley, and wine and season to taste with salt and pepper. Increase the heat to medium and bring to a boil, then reduce the heat and simmer, stirring occasionally, for 15–20 minutes, until thickened.

2. Meanwhile, scrub the mussels and clams under cold running water and pull off the beards from the mussels. Discard any with broken shells and any that refuse to close when tapped.

3. When the sauce has thickened, increase the heat and bring to a boil. Add the mussels and clams, cover, and cook, gently shaking the pan occasionally, for 3–5 minutes, until all the shells have opened. Discard any mussels and clams that remain closed. Transfer to a warmed serving dish, garnish with parsley, and serve immediately.

Serves 4–6

2 lb 4 oz/1 kg mussels

2 lb 4 oz/1 kg clams

Tomato sauce
* 1 tbsp butter
* 1 tbsp olive oil
* 1 shallot, finely chopped
* 1 garlic clove, finely chopped
* ½ celery stalk, finely chopped
* 9 oz/250 g plum tomatoes, peeled, cored, and chopped
* 1 tbsp tomato paste
* brown sugar, to taste
* 1 tbsp chopped fresh flat-leaf parsley, plus extra to garnish
  3 tbsp dry white wine
* salt and pepper

Tomato Soup

1. Melt the butter with the oil in a pan. Add the onion, garlic, and celery and cook over low heat, stirring occasionally, for 5 minutes, until softened. Stir in the tomatoes, tomato paste, and water. Increase the heat to medium and bring to a boil, then reduce the heat and simmer, stirring occasionally, for 10 minutes.

2. Increase the heat to medium, stir in sugar to taste, the basil, and stock, and season to taste with salt and pepper. Bring to a boil, then reduce the heat and simmer for an additional 10 minutes.

3. Taste and adjust the seasoning, adding salt and pepper if needed. Ladle into warmed bowls, garnish with basil, and serve immediately.

Serves 4

- ✳ 2 tbsp butter
- ✳ 2 tbsp olive oil
- ✳ 1 large onion, finely chopped
- ✳ 2 garlic cloves, finely chopped
- ✳ 1 celery stalk, finely chopped
- ✳ 1 lb 2 oz plum/500 g tomatoes, peeled, cored, and chopped
- ✳ 2 tbsp tomato paste
- ✳ scant ½ cup water
- ✳ brown sugar, to taste
- ✳ 1 tbsp chopped fresh basil, plus extra to garnish
- 1¼ cups vegetable stock
- ✳ salt and pepper

Green Beans Spanish Style

1. Melt the butter with the oil in a large pan. Add the shallots, garlic, and celery and cook over low heat, stirring occasionally, for 5 minutes, until softened. Add the beans and cook, stirring occasionally, for an additional 4 minutes.

2. Stir in the tomatoes, tomato paste, sugar to taste, chives, bay leaf, pine nuts, and lemon juice and season to taste with salt and pepper. Increase the heat to medium and bring to a boil, stirring constantly, then reduce the heat and simmer, stirring occasionally, for 25–30 minutes, until the beans are tender and the sauce has thickened.

3. Remove and discard the bay leaf. Transfer the mixture to a warmed serving dish, garnish with chives, and serve immediately.

Serves 6

- 2 tbsp butter
- 2 tbsp olive oil
- 2 shallots, finely chopped
- 2 garlic cloves, finely chopped
- 1 celery stalk, finely chopped
- 2 lb 4 oz/1 kg green beans, cut into 1-inch/2.5-cm lengths
- 1 lb 12 oz/800 g canned chopped tomatoes
- 2 tbsp tomato paste
- brown sugar, to taste
- 1 tbsp snipped fresh chives, plus extra to garnish
- 1 bay leaf
- 1 tbsp chopped pine nuts
- 1 tbsp lemon juice
- salt and pepper

Omelet Slices in Tomato & Red Wine Sauce

1. First, make the sauce. Melt the butter with the oil in a pan. Add the onion, garlic, and celery and cook over low heat, stirring occasionally, for 5 minutes, until softened. Stir in the tomatoes, tomato paste, sugar to taste, basil, and wine and season to taste with salt and pepper. Increase the heat to medium and bring to a boil, then reduce the heat and simmer, stirring occasionally, for 15–20 minutes, until thickened.

2. Meanwhile, lightly beat the eggs in a bowl and season to taste with salt and pepper. Melt the butter with the oil in a 10-inch/25-cm skillet over medium heat. Pour in the eggs and tilt and rotate the skillet to spread them evenly. Cook for a few seconds, until the bottom of the omelet begins to set. Lift the edge with a spatula and tilt the skillet so that the uncooked egg runs underneath. Continue to cook until the bottom has set and the top is just firm but still creamy. Slide the omelet out of the skillet onto a plate.

3. Cut the omelet into thick slices and transfer to a warmed serving dish. Strain the sauce over the omelet slices, turning them so that they are well coated. Garnish with basil and serve immediately.

Serves 4

8 eggs
1 tbsp butter
1 tbsp olive oil
salt and pepper

Tomato & red wine sauce
* 2 tbsp butter
* 2 tbsp olive oil
* 1 small onion, finely chopped
* 2 garlic cloves, finely chopped
* 1 celery stalk, finely chopped
* 1 lb 2 oz/500 g plum tomatoes, peeled, cored, and chopped
* 2 tbsp tomato paste
* brown sugar, to taste
* 1 tbsp chopped fresh basil, plus extra to garnish
* scant ½ cup red wine
* salt and pepper

19

Pasta in Tomato Sauce with Two Cheeses

1. First, make the sauce. Melt the butter with the oil in a pan. Add the shallots, garlic, and celery and cook over low heat, stirring occasionally, for 5 minutes, until softened. Stir in the tomatoes, tomato paste, sugar to taste, oregano, and water and season to taste with salt and pepper. Increase the heat to medium and bring to a boil, then reduce the heat and simmer, stirring occasionally, for 15–20 minutes, until thickened.

2. Meanwhile, bring a large pan of lightly salted water to a boil. Add the pasta, bring back to a boil, and cook for 8–10 minutes, until tender but still firm to the bite. Drain and return to the pan.

3. Add the sauce and both kinds of cheese to the pasta and toss well over low heat until the cheeses have melted. Transfer to a warmed serving dish and serve immediately.

Serves 4

1 lb/450 g dried penne
1 cup diced Bel Paese cheese
⅔ cup grated Parmesan cheese
salt

Tomato sauce
- 2 tbsp butter
- 2 tbsp olive oil
- 2 shallots, finely chopped
- 2 garlic cloves, finely chopped
- 1 celery stalk, finely chopped
- 14 oz/400 g canned chopped tomatoes
- 2 tbsp tomato paste
- brown sugar, to taste
- 1 tsp dried oregano
- scant ½ cup water
- salt and pepper

20

Baked Eggs with Tomato & Corn Sauce

1. Melt the butter with the oil in a pan. Add the onion, garlic, and celery and cook over low heat, stirring occasionally, for 5 minutes, until softened. Add the bacon and bell pepper and cook, stirring occasionally, for an additional 10 minutes. Stir in the tomatoes, tomato paste, sugar to taste, parsley, cayenne pepper, and water and season to taste with salt and pepper. Increase the heat to medium and bring to a boil, then reduce the heat and simmer, stirring occasionally, for 15 minutes, until thickened.

2. Meanwhile, preheat the oven to 350°F/180°C. Stir the corn into the sauce and transfer the mixture to an ovenproof dish. Make 4 small hollows with the back of a spoon and break an egg into each. Bake in the preheated oven for 25–30 minutes, until the eggs have set. Serve immediately.

Serves 4

- ✳ 2 tbsp butter
- ✳ 2 tbsp olive oil
- ✳ 1 onion, finely chopped
- ✳ 2 garlic cloves, finely chopped
- ✳ 1 celery stalk, finely chopped
- 9 slices lean bacon, chopped
- 1 red bell pepper, seeded and diced
- ✳ 1 lb 2 oz/500 g plum tomatoes, peeled, cored, and chopped
- ✳ 2 tbsp tomato paste
- ✳ brown sugar, to taste
- ✳ 1 tbsp chopped fresh parsley
- pinch of cayenne pepper
- ✳ scant ½ cup water
- 8 oz/225 g canned corn kernels, drained
- 4 extra large eggs
- ✳ salt and pepper

Grilled Cheese with Tomato Yogurt Sauce

1 First, make the sauce. Melt the butter with the oil in a pan. Add the onion and garlic and cook over low heat, stirring occasionally, for 5 minutes, until softened. Stir in the tomatoes, tomato paste, sugar to taste, and water and season to taste with salt and pepper. Increase the heat to medium and bring to a boil, then reduce the heat and simmer, stirring occasionally, for 15–20 minutes, until thickened. Remove the pan from the heat and let the sauce cool.

2 When the sauce is cold, stir in the cumin, coriander, and yogurt and set aside. Make a bed of lettuce on each of 4 serving plates.

3 Cut the cheese into 16 slices. Heat a grill pan. Cook the cheese slices for 3–4 minutes on each side, then divide them among the plates. Spoon the sauce onto the plates, sprinkle with the olives, and serve immediately.

Serves 4

12 oz/350 g provolone cheese
¾ cup pitted black olives
shredded lettuce, to serve

Tomato yogurt sauce
✳ 2 tbsp butter
✳ 2 tbsp olive oil
✳ 1 small onion, finely chopped
✳ 2 garlic cloves, finely chopped
✳ 1 lb 2 oz/500 g plum tomatoes, peeled, cored, and chopped
✳ 2 tbsp tomato paste
✳ brown sugar, to taste
✳ scant ½ cup water
  1 tbsp ground cumin
  1 tbsp ground coriander
  ⅔ cup plain yogurt
✳ salt and pepper

Zucchini & Bell Peppers in Tomato Sauce

1. Melt the butter with the oil in a large pan. Add the onion, garlic, celery, zucchini, and bell peppers and cook over low heat, stirring occasionally, for 5 minutes, until softened. Stir in the tomatoes, tomato paste, sugar to taste, basil, bay leaf, and water and season to taste with salt and pepper. Increase the heat to medium and bring to a boil, then reduce the heat and simmer, stirring occasionally, for 30 minutes, until thickened and the vegetables are tender.

2. Meanwhile, preheat the broiler. Remove and discard the bay leaf and spoon the vegetable mixture into an ovenproof dish. Sprinkle with the anchovies and Parmesan and cook under the preheated broiler for 3–5 minutes, until the top is golden brown and bubbling. Serve immediately.

Serves 4

* 2 tbsp butter
* 2 tbsp olive oil
* 1 onion, thinly sliced
* 2 garlic cloves, finely chopped
* 1 celery stalk, finely chopped
  1 lb 9 oz/700 g zucchini, sliced
  2 large red bell peppers, seeded and sliced
* 14 oz/400 g canned chopped tomatoes
* 2 tbsp tomato paste
* brown sugar, to taste
* 1 tbsp chopped fresh basil
* 1 bay leaf
* scant ½ cup water
  6 canned anchovy fillets, drained and chopped
  ⅔ cup grated Parmesan cheese
* salt and pepper

Favorite

23

Lasagna

1. Heat the oil in a large pan. Add the bacon and cook over medium heat, stirring occasionally, for 2–3 minutes. Reduce the heat to low, add the garlic and onion, and cook, stirring occasionally, for 5 minutes, until softened.

2. Add the ground beef, increase the heat to medium, and cook, stirring frequently and breaking it up with a wooden spoon, for 8–10 minutes, until evenly browned. Stir in the carrots, celery, and mushrooms and cook, stirring occasionally, for an additional 5 minutes. Add the oregano, pour in the wine and stock, and stir in the sun-dried tomato paste. Season to taste with salt and pepper. Bring to a boil, reduce the heat, and simmer for 40 minutes.

3. Preheat the oven to 375°F/190°C. Make alternating layers of the meat sauce, lasagna noodles, and Parmesan in a large, rectangular ovenproof dish. Pour the tomato sauce over the top to cover completely. Bake in the preheated oven for 30 minutes. Remove the dish from the oven and let stand for 10 minutes, then cut into squares and serve with a mixed salad.

Serves 4

2 tbsp olive oil

2 slices bacon, chopped

1 garlic clove, finely chopped

1 onion, chopped

8 oz/225 g ground beef

2 carrots, chopped

2 celery stalks, chopped

1⅔ cups chopped mushrooms

pinch of dried oregano

5 tbsp red wine

⅔ cup beef stock

1 tbsp sun-dried tomato paste

8 oz/225 g lasagna noodles, cooked according to package directions

1⅓ cups grated Parmesan cheese

✳ 1 quantity Basic Tomato Sauce (see page 10)

salt and pepper

mixed salad, to serve

24

Spaghetti & Meatballs in Tomato Sauce

1. Tear the bread into pieces, put it into a large bowl with the milk, and let soak for 5 minutes. Add the ground beef, garlic, breadcrumbs, 5 tablespoons of the Parmesan, the egg, lemon rind, and thyme and season to taste with salt and pepper. Mix well with your hands until thoroughly combined. Shape the mixture into about 30 walnut-size balls and put them on a baking sheet. Chill in the refrigerator for 30 minutes.

2. Meanwhile, pour the tomato sauce into a large saucepan and place over a low heat. Heat gently until warmed through.

3. Melt ½ cup of the butter in a skillet. Add the meatballs, in batches, and cook over medium heat, turning occasionally, for 6–8 minutes, until evenly browned. Using a slotted spoon, transfer the meatballs to the tomato sauce. When they have all been added, cover the pan and simmer for 25–30 minutes, until cooked through.

4. Meanwhile, bring a large pan of lightly salted water to a boil. Add the spaghetti, bring back to a boil, and cook for 8–10 minutes, until tender but still firm to the bite. Drain, tip into a warmed serving dish, and toss with the remaining butter. Spoon the meatballs on top and pour the sauce over them. Sprinkle with the remaining Parmesan and serve immediately.

Serves 4

2 thick slices bread, crusts removed

3 tbsp milk

2 lb 4 oz/1 kg ground beef

1 garlic clove, finely chopped

scant ½ cup dry breadcrumbs

1 cup grated Parmesan cheese

1 egg, lightly beaten

2 tsp grated lemon rind

1 tsp dried thyme

* 1 quantity Basic Tomato Sauce (see page 10)

⅔ cup butter

1 lb 2 oz/500 g dried spaghetti

salt and pepper

Veal Schnitzel with Tomato & Bitter Orange Sauce

1. Put the scallops between 2 sheets of plastic wrap and beat until thin and even. Transfer to a shallow dish and sprinkle with the lemon juice and salt and pepper to taste. Cover with plastic wrap and let marinate for 1 hour.

2. Meanwhile, make the sauce. Cut the orange rind into thin shreds and set aside. Melt the butter with the oil in a pan. Add the shallots, garlic, and celery and cook over low heat, stirring occasionally, for 5 minutes, until softened. Stir the tomatoes, tomato paste, sugar to taste, most of the orange rind, and the orange juice into the pan and season to taste with salt and pepper. Increase the heat to medium and bring to a boil, then reduce the heat and simmer, stirring occasionally, for 15–20 minutes, until thickened.

3. Lightly beat the egg in a shallow dish and spread out the breadcrumbs in a separate shallow dish. Dip the scallops first in the egg and then in the breadcrumbs to coat.

4. Melt the butter in a skillet. Add 2 scallops and cook for 3–4 minutes on each side, until golden brown and cooked through. Remove from the pan and keep warm while you cook the remaining scallops. Transfer the scallops to a warmed serving dish. Pour the sauce over them and garnish with parsley sprigs and the remaining orange rind. Serve immediately.

Serves 4

4 veal scallops
juice of 2 lemons
1 extra large egg
1⅔ cups dry breadcrumbs
3 tbsp butter
salt and pepper
fresh flat-leaf parsley sprigs, to garnish

Tomato & bitter orange sauce
thinly pared rind and juice of 2 Temple oranges (use regular oranges if Temple oranges are unavailable)
* 2 tbsp butter
* 2 tbsp olive oil
2 shallots, finely chopped
* 2 garlic cloves, finely chopped
* 1 celery stalk, finely chopped
* 1 lb 2 oz/500 g plum tomatoes, peeled, cored, and chopped
* 2 tbsp tomato paste
* brown sugar, to taste
* salt and pepper

Hawaiian Pizza

1. To make the pizza dough, sift the flour and salt into a bowl and stir in the yeast. Make a well in the center and pour in the oil and lukewarm water, then mix to a soft dough. Turn out onto a lightly floured surface and knead for 10 minutes, until smooth and elastic. Shape into a ball, put it into an oiled plastic bag, and let rise in a warm place for about 1 hour, until doubled in volume.

2. Melt the butter with the oil in a pan. Add the onion and celery and cook over low heat, stirring occasionally, for 5 minutes, until softened. Stir in the tomatoes, tomato paste, sugar to taste, oregano, and water and season to taste with salt and pepper. Increase the heat to medium and bring to a boil, then reduce the heat and simmer, stirring occasionally, for 15–20 minutes, until thickened. Remove from the heat and set aside.

3. Preheat the oven to 425°F/220°C. Brush a baking sheet with oil. Punch down the dough and knead briefly on a lightly floured surface. Roll out into a circle and transfer to the prepared baking sheet. Push up a rim all the way around.

4. Spread the tomato sauce evenly over the pizza crust. Sprinkle evenly with the ham and pineapple, then top with the cheese. Drizzle with oil and bake in the preheated oven for 15–20 minutes, until crisp and golden. Serve immediately.

Serves 2

* 2 tbsp butter
* 1 tbsp olive oil, plus extra for brushing and drizzling
* 1 small onion, finely chopped
* ½ celery stalk, finely chopped
* 7 oz/200 g canned chopped tomatoes
* 1 tbsp tomato paste
* brown sugar, to taste
* ½ tsp dried oregano
* 3 tbsp water
  1 cup diced ham
  8 oz/225 g canned pineapple chunks in juice, drained
  ½ cup grated cheddar cheese
* salt and pepper

Pizza dough
2 cups white bread flour, plus extra for dusting
1 tsp salt
½ tsp active dry yeast
1 tbsp olive oil
⅔ cup lukewarm water

27

Pepperoni & Chile Pizza

1. Melt the butter with the oil in a pan. Add the onion, garlic, and celery and cook over low heat, stirring occasionally, for 5 minutes, until softened. Stir in the canned tomatoes, tomato paste, honey, Worcestershire sauce, vinegar, mustard powder, and Tabasco and season to taste with salt and pepper. Increase the heat to medium and bring to a boil, then reduce the heat and simmer, stirring occasionally, for 15–20 minutes, until thickened. Remove from the heat and set aside.

2. Meanwhile, preheat the oven to 425°F/220°C. Brush a baking sheet with oil. Punch down the dough and knead briefly on a lightly floured surface. Roll out into a circle and transfer to the prepared baking sheet. Push up a rim all the way around.

3. Spread the tomato sauce evenly over the pizza crust and top with the tomato slices. Sprinkle with the ham, cover with the pepperoni slices, and top with the chiles. Sprinkle with the cheese, drizzle with oil, and bake in the preheated oven for 15–20 minutes, until crisp and golden. Serve immediately.

Serves 2

* 1 tbsp butter
* 1 tbsp olive oil, plus extra for brushing and drizzling
* 1 small onion, finely chopped
* 1 garlic clove, finely chopped
* 1 celery stalk, finely chopped
* 7 oz/200 g canned chopped tomatoes
* 1 tbsp tomato paste
1½ tbsp honey
1 tbsp Worcestershire sauce
1½ tsp white wine vinegar
½ tsp mustard powder
dash of Tabasco sauce
1 quantity Pizza Dough (see page 66)
all-purpose flour, for dusting
4 tomatoes, sliced
generous ½ cup diced smoked ham
1 cup thinly sliced pepperoni sausage
2 fresh red chiles, thinly sliced
½ cup grated cheddar cheese
* salt and pepper

Spareribs in Barbecue Sauce

1 Preheat the oven to 400°F/200°C. Melt the butter with the oil in a pan. Add the onion, garlic, and celery and cook over low heat, stirring occasionally, for 5 minutes, until softened. Stir in the tomatoes, tomato paste, sugar, orange juice, honey, mustard, vinegar, and Worcestershire sauce and season to taste with salt and pepper. Increase the heat to medium and bring to a boil, then reduce the heat and simmer, stirring occasionally, for 15–20 minutes, until thickened. Remove the pan from the heat.

2 Spread out the spareribs in a shallow roasting pan and bake in the preheated oven for 25 minutes. Remove from the oven and spoon half the sauce over them. Reduce the oven temperature to 350°F/180°C, return the pan to the oven, and cook for an additional 20 minutes.

3 Remove the pan from the oven and turn the ribs over. Spoon the remaining sauce over them and return the pan to the oven. Cook for an additional 25–30 minutes, until the meat is tender. Garnish with parsley and serve immediately.

Serves 4

* 2 tbsp butter
* 2 tbsp olive oil
* 1 onion, finely chopped
* 2 garlic cloves, finely chopped
* 1 celery stalk, finely chopped
* 14 oz/400 g canned chopped tomatoes
* 2 tbsp tomato paste
* 2–3 tbsp brown sugar
  2 tbsp orange juice
  1 tbsp honey
  1 tsp whole grain mustard
  2 tbsp red wine vinegar
  1 tbsp Worcestershire sauce
  3 lb 5 oz/1.5 kg pork spareribs
* salt and pepper
  chopped fresh flat-leaf parsley, to garnish

29

Italian Pork Scallops

1. First, make the sauce. Melt the butter with the oil in a pan. Add the onion, garlic, and celery and cook over low heat, stirring occasionally, for 5 minutes, until softened. Stir in the tomatoes, tomato paste, sugar to taste, basil, bay leaf, and wine and season to taste with salt and pepper. Increase the heat to medium and bring to a boil, then reduce the heat and simmer, stirring occasionally, for 15–20 minutes, until thickened.

2. Preheat the broiler. Put the scallops between 2 sheets of plastic wrap and beat with a meat mallet or the side of a rolling pin until thin and even. Season well with pepper.

3. Heat the oil in a skillet. Add 2 scallops and cook over medium–high heat for 1–1½ minutes on each side, until golden brown. Transfer to a large flameproof dish. Cook the remaining scallops in the same way and transfer to the dish.

4. Remove and discard the bay leaf from the sauce, then spread the sauce evenly over the scallops. Sprinkle with the basil and top with the mozzarella cheese. Cook under the preheated broiler for 1–2 minutes, until the cheese has melted. Serve immediately.

Serves 4

4 pork scallops, about
    4 oz/115 g each
2 tbsp olive oil
2 tbsp chopped fresh basil
3 oz/85 g mozzarella cheese,
    thinly sliced
pepper

Tomato sauce
2 tbsp butter
2 tbsp olive oil
1 red onion, finely chopped
2 garlic cloves, finely chopped
1 celery stalk, finely chopped
14 oz/400 g canned chopped
    tomatoes
2 tbsp tomato paste
brown sugar, to taste
2 tbsp chopped fresh basil
1 bay leaf
scant ½ cup dry white wine
salt and pepper

30

Ham Steaks with Tomato & Sage Sauce

1. First, make the sauce. Melt the butter with the oil in a pan. Add the onions, garlic, celery, and bell pepper and cook over low heat, stirring occasionally, for 5 minutes, until softened. Stir in the tomatoes, tomato paste, sugar to taste, chopped sage, and water and season to taste with salt and pepper. Increase the heat to medium and bring to a boil, then reduce the heat and simmer, stirring occasionally, for 25–30 minutes, until thickened.

2. Preheat the broiler. Season the ham steaks with pepper and rub with the dried sage. Cook under the preheated broiler for 5 minutes on each side, until tender and cooked through. Transfer the ham steaks to warmed serving plates, spoon the sauce over them, and serve immediately.

Serves 4

4 ham steaks
1 tsp dried sage
pepper

Tomato & sage sauce
* 2 tbsp butter
* 2 tbsp olive oil
* 2 large onions, thinly sliced
* 2 garlic cloves, finely chopped
* 1 celery stalk, finely chopped
1 green bell pepper, seeded and cut into julienne strips
* 1 lb 12 oz/800 g canned chopped tomatoes
* 3 tbsp tomato paste
* brown sugar, to taste
* 1 tbsp chopped fresh sage
* scant ½ cup water
* salt and pepper

Cannelloni with Chicken & Ham

1 First, make the sauce. Melt the butter with the oil in a pan. Add the onion, garlic, and celery and cook over low heat, stirring occasionally, for 5 minutes, until softened. Stir in the tomatoes, tomato paste, sugar to taste, parsley, and water and season to taste with salt and pepper. Increase the heat to medium and bring to a boil, then reduce the heat and simmer, stirring occasionally, for 20–30 minutes, until thickened.

2 Preheat the oven to 375°F/190°C. Brush an ovenproof dish with oil. Heat the oil in a skillet, add the onion, and cook over low heat, stirring occasionally, for 5 minutes, until softened. Add the chicken and cook, stirring frequently, for an additional few minutes, until lightly browned. Remove the skillet from the heat, stir in the ham and cream cheese, and season to taste with salt and pepper.

3 Fill the cannelloni tubes with the chicken mixture and put them into the prepared dish. Pour the sauce over them, sprinkle with the Parmesan, and bake in the preheated oven for 35–40 minutes. Serve immediately.

Serves 4

1 tbsp olive oil, plus extra for brushing

1 small onion, finely chopped

6 oz/175 g ground chicken

⅔ cup finely chopped ham

⅓ cup cream cheese with garlic and herbs

8 cannelloni tubes, cooked according to the package directions

4 tbsp grated Parmesan cheese

salt and pepper

Tomato sauce
- 2 tbsp butter
- 2 tbsp olive oil
- 1 onion, finely chopped
- 2 garlic cloves, finely chopped
- 1 celery stalk, finely chopped
- 14 oz/400 g canned chopped tomatoes
- 2 tbsp tomato paste
- brown sugar, to taste
- 1 tbsp chopped fresh flat-leaf parsley
- scant ½ cup water
- salt and pepper

Barbecued Chicken

① First, make the sauce. Melt the butter with the oil in a pan. Add the onion, garlic, celery, and ginger and cook over low heat, stirring occasionally, for 5 minutes, until softened. Stir in the tomatoes, tomato paste, Worcestershire sauce, vinegar, lemon juice, sugar, oregano, bay leaf, nutmeg, and water and season to taste with salt and pepper. Increase the heat to medium and bring to a boil, then reduce the heat and simmer, stirring occasionally, for 30–40 minutes, until thickened.

② Meanwhile, preheat the barbecue or broiler. Brush the skin sides of the chicken halves with half the oil and put them skin-side down on the barbecue grill or skin-side uppermost on the broiler rack. Cook on the barbecue or under the preheated broiler for 10 minutes, then brush with the remaining oil, turn them over, and cook for an additional 20 minutes, until golden brown.

③ Brush the chicken with half the sauce. Continue to cook, turning and brushing frequently with the remaining sauce, for 15–20 minutes, until cooked through and tender. Transfer to a warmed serving dish and serve immediately.

Serves 4

2 double poussins or spring chickens, about 2 lb/ 900 g each, cut in half
4 tbsp olive oil

Barbecue sauce
✳ 2 tbsp butter
✳ 2 tbsp olive oil
✳ 1 onion, finely chopped
✳ 2 garlic cloves, finely chopped
✳ 1 celery stalk, finely chopped
½-inch/1-cm piece fresh ginger, finely chopped
✳ 14 oz/400 g canned chopped tomatoes
✳ 2 tbsp tomato paste
1 tbsp Worcestershire sauce
2 tbsp red wine vinegar
2 tbsp lemon juice
✳ 1 tbsp brown sugar
✳ 1 tsp dried oregano
✳ 1 bay leaf
pinch of grated nutmeg
✳ 2 tbsp water
✳ salt and pepper

33

Chicken Strips with Tomato & Honey Dipping Sauce

1. First, make the sauce. Melt the butter with the olive oil in a pan. Add the onion, garlic, and celery and cook over low heat, stirring occasionally, for 5 minutes, until softened. Stir in the tomatoes, tomato paste, cinnamon, ginger, and water and season to taste with salt and pepper. Increase the heat to medium and bring to a boil, then reduce the heat and simmer, stirring occasionally, for 40–50 minutes, until very thick.

2. Put the chicken between 2 sheets of plastic wrap and beat until thin and even. Cut the chicken into 1 inch/2.5 cm wide strips. Combine the breadcrumbs, coriander, cumin, and turmeric in a shallow dish and season to taste with salt and pepper. Spread out the flour in a separate shallow dish and lightly beat the egg in a third shallow dish. Toss the chicken strips, 1 at a time, first in the flour, then in the egg, and, finally, in the breadcrumb mixture.

3. Heat enough peanut oil for deep-frying in a deep-fat fryer to 350–375°F/180–190°C, or until a cube of bread browns in 30 seconds. Add the chicken strips to the hot oil, in batches, and cook until golden brown and crisp. Drain on paper towels and keep warm.

4. Stir the honey into the sauce and cook for 1 minute. Add the sesame seeds and pour the sauce into a small bowl. Serve the chicken strips immediately with the sauce.

Serves 4

2 skinless, boneless chicken breasts, about 6 oz/ 175 g each
1½ cups fresh breadcrumbs
½ tsp ground coriander
¼ tsp ground cumin
¼ tsp ground turmeric
2 tbsp all-purpose flour
1 egg
peanut oil, for deep-frying
salt and pepper

Tomato & honey sauce
2 tbsp butter
2 tbsp olive oil
1 onion, finely chopped
2 garlic cloves, finely chopped
1 celery stalk, finely chopped
1 lb 2 oz/500 g plum tomatoes, peeled, cored, and chopped
2 tbsp tomato paste
1 tsp ground cinnamon
pinch of ground ginger
scant ½ cup water
2 tbsp honey
1 tsp toasted sesame seeds
salt and pepper

Turkey Scallops with Tomato & Apple Sauce

1. First, make the sauce. Melt the butter with the olive oil in a pan. Add the shallots and apple and cook over low heat, stirring occasionally, for 5 minutes, until softened. Stir in the tomatoes, tomato paste, sugar to taste, nutmeg, and water and season to taste with salt and pepper. Increase the heat to medium and bring to a boil, then reduce the heat and simmer, stirring occasionally, for 15–20 minutes, until thickened. Remove the sauce from the heat and let cool slightly.

2. Put the turkey between 2 sheets of plastic wrap and beat until thin and even. Put the flour into a shallow dish and season to taste with salt and pepper. Lightly beat the egg in a separate shallow dish and spread out the breadcrumbs in a third shallow dish.

3. Dip the scallops, 1 at a time, first in the flour, then in the egg, and, finally, in the breadcrumbs to coat. Melt the butter with the sunflower oil in a large skillet. Add the scallops, in batches, and cook over medium heat for 1 minute on each side, until golden brown. Reduce the heat and cook for an additional 3–4 minutes on each side, until cooked through and tender.

4. Meanwhile, gently reheat the sauce. Transfer the scallops to warmed individual plates and pour the sauce over them. Garnish with parsley and serve immediately.

Serves 4

4 turkey scallops

3 tbsp all-purpose flour

1 egg

¾ cup dry breadcrumbs

4 tbsp butter

2 tbsp sunflower oil

salt and pepper

chopped fresh flat-leaf parsley, to garnish

Tomato & apple sauce

2 tbsp butter

2 tbsp olive oil

2 shallots, finely chopped

1 apple, peeled, cored, and diced

14 oz/400 g canned chopped tomatoes

2 tbsp tomato paste

brown sugar, to taste

pinch of grated nutmeg

scant ½ cup water

salt and pepper

Fish Baked in Tomato Sauce

1. First, make the sauce. Melt the butter with the oil in a pan. Add the shallots, garlic, and celery and cook over low heat, stirring occasionally, for 5 minutes, until softened. Stir in the tomatoes, tomato paste, sugar to taste, parsley, and wine and season to taste with salt and pepper. Increase the heat to medium and bring to a boil, then reduce the heat and simmer, stirring occasionally, for 15–20 minutes, until thickened.

2. Meanwhile, preheat the oven to 375°F/190°C. Grease an ovenproof dish with butter. Put the fish into the prepared dish in a single layer. Spoon the sauce over the fish steaks and sprinkle with the breadcrumbs.

3. Bake in the preheated oven, spooning the cooking juices over the fish 2–3 times, for 20–30 minutes, until the topping is crisp and golden brown. Serve immediately.

Serves 4

butter, for greasing
4 white fish steaks
2 tbsp dry breadcrumbs

Tomato sauce
* 2 tbsp butter
* 2 tbsp olive oil
2 shallots, finely chopped
* 2 garlic cloves, finely chopped
* 1 celery stalk, finely chopped
* 14 oz/400 g canned chopped tomatoes
* 2 tbsp tomato paste
* brown sugar, to taste
* 2 tbsp chopped fresh parsley
scant ½ cup dry white wine
* salt and pepper

36

Crab Cakes with Rich Tomato Sauce

1. Peel both kinds of potatoes and cut into chunks. Cook in a large pan of salted boiling water for 15–20 minutes, until tender but not falling apart. Drain well, return to the pan, and mash coarsely, then let cool.

2. Stir the egg into the cooled potatoes, then stir in the crabmeat, flour, mustard powder, and tarragon. Season to taste with salt and pepper. Lightly flour your hands, scoop up 2 tablespoons of the mixture, and shape into a patty. Repeat, flouring your hands as required, until all the mixture has been used up. Put the crab cakes on a baking sheet and chill in the refrigerator for 30 minutes to firm up.

3. Meanwhile, make the sauce. Melt the butter with 2 tablespoons of oil from the jar of sun-dried tomatoes in a pan. Add the shallots, garlic, and celery and cook over low heat, stirring occasionally, for 5 minutes, until softened. Stir in the fresh tomatoes, sun-dried tomatoes, sun-dried tomato paste, sugar to taste, tarragon, and wine. Season to taste with salt and pepper. Increase the heat to medium and bring to a boil, then reduce the heat and simmer, stirring occasionally, for 15–20 minutes, until thickened.

4. Heat the sunflower oil in a large skillet. Add the crab cakes, in batches, and cook for 2–3 minutes on each side, until golden brown and heated through. Serve immediately with the sauce and lemon wedges for squeezing over.

Serves 4

1 large potato

2 sweet potatoes

1 egg, lightly beaten

10 oz/280 g white crabmeat, thawed if frozen

2 tbsp all-purpose flour, plus extra for dusting

1 tbsp mustard powder

2 tsp chopped fresh tarragon

4 tbsp sunflower oil

salt and pepper

lemon wedges, to serve

Rich tomato sauce

2 tbsp butter

4 sun-dried tomatoes in oil, drained and chopped

2 shallots, finely chopped

2 garlic cloves, finely chopped

1 celery stalk, finely chopped

1 lb 2 oz/500 g plum tomatoes, peeled, cored, and chopped

2 tbsp sun-dried tomato paste

brown sugar, to taste

1 tbsp chopped fresh tarragon

scant ½ cup dry white wine

salt and pepper

Shrimp Fritters with Roasted Tomato Sauce

1. If the shrimp are very large, cut them in half. Put them into a bowl and sprinkle with the lemon juice and olive oil. Season to taste with salt and pepper and let marinate for 1 hour.

2. Meanwhile, make the batter. Sift flour and salt into a bowl. Add the eggs and water and beat until smooth. Cover and set aside to rest.

3. Preheat the oven to 425°F/220°C. To make the sauce, put the onion, garlic, tomatoes, sugar, and vinegar into a large ovenproof dish and drizzle with the olive oil. Roast in the preheated oven, stirring occasionally, for 30–35 minutes, until the vegetables are soft.

4. Remove the dish from the oven and let cool slightly, then transfer to a food processor or blender and process until smooth. Scrape the sauce into a clean pan, stir in the parsley, and season to taste with salt and pepper.

5. Stir the batter, then stir in the shrimp. Heat enough peanut oil for deep-frying in a deep-fat fryer to 170°C/340°F, or until a cube of bread browns in 1 minute. Meanwhile, gently reheat the sauce. Add spoonfuls of the shrimp mixture to the hot oil and cook for 4–5 minutes, until crisp and golden brown. Remove with a slotted spoon and drain on paper towels. Transfer the shrimp fritters to a warmed serving dish and pour the sauce into a serving bowl. Serve immediately.

Serves 4

1 lb 2 oz/500 g shrimp, peeled and deveined
2 tbsp lemon juice
2 tbsp olive oil
peanut oil, for deep-frying
salt and pepper

Batter
1 cup all-purpose flour
pinch of salt
2 eggs
⅔ cup water

Roasted tomato sauce
1 large onion, chopped
3 garlic cloves, chopped
1 lb 2 oz/500 g plum tomatoes, peeled, cored, and chopped
2 tbsp brown sugar
2 tbsp red wine vinegar
2 tbsp olive oil
1 tbsp chopped fresh flat-leaf parsley
salt and pepper

Margherita Pizza

1. Melt the butter with the oil in a pan. Add the onion, garlic, and celery and cook over low heat, stirring occasionally, for 5 minutes, until softened. Stir in the canned tomatoes, tomato paste, sugar to taste, basil, and water and season to taste with salt and pepper. Increase the heat to medium and bring to a boil, then reduce the heat and simmer, stirring occasionally, for 15–20 minutes, until thickened. Remove from the heat and set aside.

2. Meanwhile, preheat the oven to 425°F/220°C. Brush a baking sheet with oil. Punch down the dough and knead briefly on a lightly floured surface. Roll out into a circle and transfer to the prepared baking sheet. Push up a rim all the way around.

3. Spread the tomato sauce evenly over the pizza crust. Arrange the mozzarella and tomato slices alternately on top. Coarsely tear the basil leaves and put them on the pizza, then sprinkle with the Parmesan. Drizzle with oil and bake in the preheated oven for 15–20 minutes, until crisp and golden. Serve immediately.

Serves 2

* 1 tbsp butter
* 1 tbsp olive oil, plus extra for brushing and drizzling
* 1 small onion, finely chopped
* 1 garlic clove, finely chopped
* ½ celery stalk, finely chopped
* 7 oz/200 g canned chopped tomatoes
* 1 tbsp tomato paste
* brown sugar, to taste
* 1 tbsp chopped fresh basil
* 3 tbsp water
  1 quantity Pizza Dough (see page 66)
  all-purpose flour, for dusting
  5 oz/140 g mozzarella cheese, sliced
  4 tomatoes, sliced
  1 fresh basil sprig
  2 tbsp grated Parmesan cheese
* salt and pepper

Vegetables à la Greece

1. Melt the butter with the oil in a pan. Add the onion, garlic, and celery and cook over low heat, stirring occasionally, for 5 minutes, until softened. Stir in the tomatoes, tomato paste, sugar to taste, wine, lemon juice, and parsley and season to taste with salt and pepper. Increase the heat to medium and bring to a boil, then reduce the heat and simmer, stirring occasionally, for 15–20 minutes, until thickened.

2. Add the shallots and cauliflower and simmer for 10 minutes, then stir in the mushrooms and simmer for an additional 5 minutes.

3. Using a slotted spoon, transfer the shallots, cauliflower, and mushrooms to a serving dish. Increase the heat to medium–high and cook the sauce, stirring constantly, until reduced and thickened. Remove from the heat and pour it over the vegetables.

4. Let cool, then cover and chill in the refrigerator for at least 2 hours before serving.

Serves 4

* 2 tbsp butter
* 2 tbsp olive oil
* 1 onion, finely chopped
* 2 garlic cloves, finely chopped
* 1 celery stalk, finely chopped
* 1 lb 2 oz/500 g plum tomatoes, peeled, cored, and chopped
* 2 tbsp tomato paste
* brown sugar, to taste
  ⅔ cup dry white wine
  1 tbsp lemon juice
* 1 tbsp chopped fresh parsley
  8 shallots, trimmed and peeled
  1½ cups cauliflower florets
  8 white mushrooms
* salt and pepper

Baked Eggplant with Tomato Sauce & Parmesan

① First, make the sauce. Melt the butter with the oil in a pan. Add the onion, garlic, and celery and cook over low heat, stirring occasionally, for 5 minutes, until softened. Stir in the tomatoes, tomato paste, sugar to taste, basil, oregano, and water and season to taste with salt and pepper. Increase the heat to medium and bring to a boil, then reduce the heat and simmer, stirring occasionally, for 15–20 minutes, until thickened.

② Meanwhile, preheat the oven to 450°F/230°C. Grease a baking sheet with butter. Melt the butter and pour it into a shallow dish. Spread out the breadcrumbs in a separate shallow dish. Dip the eggplant slices first in the melted butter and then in the breadcrumbs to coat. Put them on the prepared baking sheet and season to taste with salt. Bake in the preheated oven for 20 minutes, until golden brown and tender.

③ Remove the baking sheet from the oven. Top each eggplant slice with a spoonful of tomato sauce and sprinkle with a little of the oregano and Parmesan. Return to the oven and bake for an additional 10 minutes, until the topping is golden brown. Transfer to a serving dish, garnish with basil, and serve immediately.

Serves 6

3 tbsp butter, plus extra for greasing
⅔ cup dry breadcrumbs
1 large eggplant, cut into ½-inch/1-cm slices
1 tsp dried oregano
⅔ cup grated Parmesan cheese
salt

Tomato sauce
✳ 2 tbsp butter
✳ 2 tbsp olive oil
✳ 1 small onion, finely chopped
✳ 1 garlic clove, finely chopped
✳ 1 celery stalk, finely chopped
✳ 14 oz/400 g canned chopped tomatoes
✳ 2 tbsp tomato paste
✳ brown sugar, to taste
✳ 1 tbsp chopped fresh basil, plus extra to garnish
✳ 1 tsp dried oregano
✳ scant ½ cup water
✳ salt and pepper

41

Fettuccine with Tomato & Mushroom Sauce

1. First, make the sauce. Melt the butter with the oil in a pan. Add the onion, garlic, and celery and cook over low heat, stirring occasionally, for 5 minutes, until softened. Stir in the tomatoes, tomato paste, wine, and mushrooms. Increase the heat to medium and bring to a boil, then reduce the heat and simmer, stirring occasionally, for 15–20 minutes, until thickened.

2. Meanwhile, bring a large pan of lightly salted water to a boil. Add the fettuccine, bring back to a boil, and cook for 8–10 minutes, until tender but still firm to the bite. Drain, turn into a warmed serving dish, and toss with the butter.

3. Stir sugar to taste and the basil into the sauce and season to taste with salt and pepper. Pour the sauce over the pasta, toss well, and sprinkle with the Parmesan. Serve immediately.

Serves 4

1 lb/450 g dried fettuccine
1 tbsp butter
2 tbsp grated Parmesan cheese
salt

Tomato & mushroom sauce
* 2 tbsp butter
* 2 tbsp olive oil
* 1 large onion, finely chopped
* 2 garlic cloves, finely chopped
* 1 celery stalk, finely chopped
* 14 oz/400 g canned chopped tomatoes
* 2 tbsp tomato paste
  4 tbsp dry red wine
  1⅔ cups sliced mushrooms
* brown sugar, to taste
* 1 tbsp chopped fresh basil
* salt and pepper

42

Tomato Soufflé

① Cook the potatoes in a large pan of salted boiling water for 20–25 minutes, until tender but not falling apart. Drain well and set aside.

② Meanwhile, make the sauce. Melt the butter with the oil in a pan. Add the onion, garlic, and celery and cook over low heat, stirring occasionally, for 5 minutes, until softened. Stir in the canned tomatoes, tomato paste, sugar to taste, ginger, bay leaf, and water and season to taste with salt and pepper. Increase the heat to medium and bring to a boil, then reduce the heat and simmer, stirring occasionally, for 15–20 minutes, until thickened.

③ Preheat the oven to 450°F/230°C. Brush a 7-cup soufflé dish with oil and dust with flour, tipping out the excess. Remove the sauce from the heat and let cool slightly. Remove and discard the bay leaf. Pour the sauce into a food processor, add the potatoes, and process to a smooth paste. Transfer to a bowl and stir in the diced tomato, egg yolk, and oil. Taste and adjust the seasoning, adding salt and pepper if needed.

④ Whisk the egg whites in a grease-free bowl until they form soft peaks. Stir one-quarter of the egg whites into the tomato mixture, then fold in the remainder. Pour into the prepared dish and bake in the preheated oven for 35–40 minutes, until risen and golden brown. Serve immediately.

Serves 4

2 potatoes, cut into chunks

all-purpose flour, for dusting

1 beefsteak tomato, peeled, seeded, and diced

1 egg yolk

1 tbsp olive oil, plus extra for brushing

5 egg whites

salt and pepper

Tomato sauce

✳ 2 tbsp butter

✳ 3 tbsp olive oil

✳ 1 onion, finely chopped

✳ 2 garlic cloves, finely chopped

✳ 1 celery stalk, finely chopped

✳ 14 oz/400 g canned chopped tomatoes

✳ 2 tbsp tomato paste

✳ brown sugar, to taste

1 tsp chopped fresh ginger

✳ 1 bay leaf

✳ scant ½ cup water

✳ salt and pepper

43

Special Macaroni & Cheese

1. First, make the sauce. Melt the butter with the oil in a pan. Add the onion, garlic, and celery and cook over low heat, stirring occasionally, for 5 minutes, until softened. Stir in the tomatoes, tomato paste, sugar to taste, basil, and water and season to taste with salt and pepper. Increase the heat to medium and bring to a boil, then reduce the heat and simmer, stirring occasionally, for 15–20 minutes, until thickened.

2. Meanwhile, preheat the oven to 375°F/190°C. Grease an ovenproof dish with butter. Bring a large pan of lightly salted water to a boil. Add the macaroni, bring back to a boil, and cook for 8–10 minutes, until tender but still firm to the bite. Drain well.

3. Combine the Parmesan and Gruyère cheeses in a bowl. Spoon one-third of the tomato sauce into the prepared dish, cover with one-third of the macaroni, and sprinkle with one-third of the mixed cheeses. Repeat twice. Combine the breadcrumbs and basil and sprinkle over the top. Dot with the butter and bake in the preheated oven for 20–25 minutes, until the topping is golden brown. Serve immediately.

Serves 4

8 oz/225 g dried macaroni

1⅓ cups grated Parmesan cheese

1½ cups grated Gruyère cheese

½ cup fresh breadcrumbs

1 tbsp chopped fresh basil

1 tbsp butter, plus extra for greasing

salt

Tomato sauce

※ 2 tbsp butter

※ 2 tbsp olive oil

※ 1 small onion, finely chopped

※ 2 garlic cloves, finely chopped

※ 1 celery stalk, finely chopped

※ 14 oz/400 g canned chopped tomatoes

※ 2 tbsp tomato paste

※ brown sugar, to taste

※ 1 tbsp chopped fresh basil

※ scant ½ cup water

※ salt and pepper

Spicy

44

Beef Enchiladas in Piquant Tomato Sauce

1. Heat the corn oil in a skillet. Add the onion and chiles and cook over low heat, stirring occasionally, for 5 minutes. Add the ground beef, increase the heat to medium, and cook, stirring frequently and breaking it up with a wooden spoon, for 8–10 minutes, until evenly browned. Remove the pan from the heat and stir in half the cheese.

2. To make the sauce, melt the butter with the olive oil in a pan. Add the onion, garlic, and chile and cook over medium heat, stirring occasionally, for 5–8 minutes, until the onion is golden brown. Stir in the tomatoes, tomato paste, sugar to taste, oregano, and cayenne pepper and season to taste with salt and pepper. Increase the heat to medium and bring to a boil. Reduce the heat, stir in the cream, and simmer, stirring occasionally, for 15–20 minutes, until thickened. Remove from the heat and let cool slightly.

3. Meanwhile, preheat the oven to 350°F/180°C. Heat a skillet and brush with corn oil. Dip the tortillas, 1 at a time, in the sauce, shake off any excess, and cook for 30 seconds on each side. Transfer to a large plate, put a tablespoon of the meat mixture in the center, and roll up. Put the filled tortillas, seam-side down, in a large ovenproof dish and pour the remaining sauce over them. Sprinkle with the remaining cheese and bake in the preheated oven for 15–20 minutes. Garnish with cilantro and serve immediately.

Serves 6

1 tbsp corn oil, plus extra for brushing

1 onion, finely chopped

2 fresh green chiles, seeded and chopped

10 oz/280 g ground beef

1 cup grated cheddar cheese

18 flour tortillas

chopped fresh cilantro, to garnish

Piquant tomato sauce

✳ 2 tbsp butter

✳ 2 tbsp olive oil

✳ 1 onion, finely chopped

✳ 2 garlic cloves, finely chopped

1 fresh green chile, seeded and chopped

✳ 14 oz/400 g canned chopped tomatoes

✳ 2 tbsp tomato paste

✳ brown sugar, to taste

✳ 1 tsp dried oregano

½ tsp cayenne pepper

½ cup heavy cream

✳ salt and pepper

Steak with Tomato & Horseradish Sauce

1. First, make the sauce. Melt the butter with the oil in a pan. Add the onion, garlic, and celery and cook over low heat, stirring occasionally, for 5 minutes, until softened. Stir in the tomatoes, tomato paste, horseradish, parsley, and water and season to taste with salt and pepper. Increase the heat to medium and bring to a boil, then reduce the heat and simmer, stirring occasionally, for 15–20 minutes, until thickened.

2. Meanwhile, preheat the broiler to high. Brush the steaks with oil and season well with salt and pepper.

3. Cook the steaks under the preheated broiler for 2–3 minutes on each side for rare or for 3–4 minutes on each side for medium. For well done, cook under the preheated broiler for 3 minutes on each side, then reduce the heat and broil for an additional 5 minutes on each side. Transfer to warmed plates, spoon the sauce over them, and serve immediately.

Serves 6

6 sirloin steaks, about 8 oz/ 225 g each

olive oil, for brushing

salt and pepper

Tomato & horseradish sauce
* 2 tbsp butter
* 2 tbsp olive oil
* 1 onion, finely chopped
* 2 garlic cloves, finely chopped
* 1 celery stalk, finely chopped
* 14 oz/400 g canned chopped tomatoes
* 2 tbsp tomato paste
  2 tbsp creamed horseradish
* 2 tbsp chopped fresh flat-leaf parsley
* scant ½ cup water
* salt and pepper

Spicy Meatballs

1. First, make the meatballs. Mix together the pork, grated onion, garlic, breadcrumbs, almonds, egg, cinnamon, and sherry, kneading with you hands until thoroughly combined. Shape the mixture into 36 walnut-size balls.

2. Heat the oil in a skillet. Add the meatballs, in batches, and cook over medium heat, turning frequently, for 6–8 minutes, until evenly browned. Remove with a slotted spoon, set aside, and keep warm.

3. Add the chopped onion, garlic, and sugar to the skillet and cook over low heat, stirring occasionally, for 8–10 minutes, until the onion is golden brown. Add the tomatoes, bell peppers, chiles, tomato paste, cilantro, and paprika and cook, stirring occasionally, for an additional 5 minutes. Pour in ⅔ cup of the stock and season to taste with salt and pepper, then increase the heat and bring to a boil.

4. Meanwhile, mix the cornstarch to a paste with the remaining stock in a bowl. Reduce the heat, stir in the cornstarch mixture, and add the meatballs. Cover and simmer for 20–25 minutes, until the meatballs are cooked through. Transfer to a warmed serving dish, garnish with cilantro, and serve immediately.

Serves 6

- 3 tbsp corn oil
- 1 large onion, finely chopped
- 1 garlic clove, finely chopped
- 1 tbsp brown sugar
- 14 oz/400 g canned chopped tomatoes
- 1 red and 1 green bell pepper, seeded and sliced
- 2 fresh green chiles, chopped
- 2 tbsp tomato paste
- 1 tbsp chopped fresh cilantro, plus extra to garnish
- 1 tsp paprika
- scant 1 cup chicken stock
- 2 tsp cornstarch
- salt and pepper

Meatballs
- 2 lb 4 oz/1 kg ground pork
- 1 large onion, grated
- 2 garlic cloves, finely chopped
- 1 cup fresh breadcrumbs
- ½ cup ground almonds
- 1 egg, lightly beaten
- 1 tsp ground cinnamon
- 3 tbsp dry sherry

Pork Chops Mexican Style

① Rub the pork chops all over with the cut sides of the garlic. Put them on a plate, cover with plastic wrap, and chill in the refrigerator for 4 hours.

② Meanwhile, make the sauce. Melt the butter with the olive oil in a pan. Add the onion, garlic, and celery and cook over low heat, stirring occasionally, for 5 minutes, until softened. Stir in the tomatoes, tomato paste, sugar to taste, chiles, and water and season to taste with salt and pepper. Increase the heat to medium and bring to a boil, then reduce the heat and simmer, stirring occasionally, for 20 minutes. Remove from the heat and let cool slightly, then transfer to a food processor or blender and process to a paste.

③ Heat the corn oil in a large skillet. Add the chops and cook over medium heat for 5 minutes on each side, until evenly browned. Pour in the sauce, reduce the heat, cover, and simmer, turning the chops once or twice, for 15–20 minutes, until cooked through and tender.

④ Meanwhile, peel, pit, and slice the avocado, then sprinkle with the lime juice to prevent discoloration. When the chops are ready, transfer to a warmed serving dish, pour the sauce over them, and top with the avocado. Serve immediately.

Serves 4

4 pork chops
2 garlic cloves, halved
2 tbsp corn oil
1 avocado
2 tbsp lime juice

Tomato & chile sauce
✳ 2 tbsp butter
✳ 2 tbsp olive oil
✳ 1 onion, finely chopped
✳ 2 garlic cloves, finely chopped
✳ 1 celery stalk, finely chopped
✳ 1 lb 7 oz/650 g plum tomatoes, peeled, cored, and chopped
✳ 2 tbsp tomato paste
✳ brown sugar, to taste
  3 fresh green chiles, finely chopped
✳ 1¼ cups water
✳ salt and pepper

Loin of Pork with Spicy Tomato Sauce

1. First, make the sauce. Melt the butter with the olive oil in a pan. Add the onion, garlic, and celery and cook over low heat, stirring occasionally, for 5 minutes, until softened. Stir in the tomatoes, tomato paste, soy sauce, chili sauce, Worcestershire sauce, vinegar, mustard, sugar to taste, and bay leaf. Increase the heat to medium and bring to a boil, then reduce the heat and simmer, stirring occasionally, for 15–20 minutes, until thickened.

2. Meanwhile, preheat the oven to 350°F/180°C. Combine the sugar, ginger, and cayenne in a small bowl and stir in a pinch each of salt and pepper. Rub the mixture all over the pork.

3. Heat the sunflower oil in a large flameproof casserole. Add the pork and cook over medium heat, turning frequently, until evenly browned. Drain off the oil. Pour the sauce over the pork, cover the casserole, and transfer to the preheated oven. Cook, occasionally spooning the sauce over the meat, for 1¾ hours.

4. Remove the meat from the casserole, cover with aluminum foil, and let rest. Meanwhile, bring the sauce to a boil over medium heat. Skim off any fat. Cut the pork into slices and put them on a warmed serving dish. Remove and discard the bay leaf, then strain the sauce over the pork slices, pressing down with the back of a spoon. Garnish with sage and serve immediately.

Serves 6

1 tbsp brown sugar
½ tsp ground ginger
½ tsp cayenne pepper
4 lb/1.8 kg boned and rolled loin of pork
2 tbsp sunflower oil
salt and pepper
chopped fresh sage, to garnish

Spicy tomato sauce
* 2 tbsp butter
* 2 tbsp olive oil
* 1 onion, finely chopped
* 2 garlic cloves, finely chopped
* 1 celery stalk, finely chopped
* 14 oz/400 g canned chopped tomatoes
* 2 tbsp tomato paste
  2 tbsp light soy sauce
  2 tbsp chili sauce
  2 tbsp Worcestershire sauce
  1 tbsp white wine vinegar
  2 tsp Dijon mustard
* brown sugar, to taste
* 1 bay leaf

Lamb Steaks with Sweet & Spicy Tomato Sauce

1. First, make the sauce. Melt the butter with the oil in a pan. Add the shallots, garlic, celery, and bell pepper and cook over low heat, stirring occasionally, for 5 minutes, until softened. Stir in the tomatoes, tomato paste, mustard, honey, sugar, chile flakes, cayenne pepper, paprika, and water and season to taste with salt and pepper. Increase the heat to medium and bring to a boil, then reduce the heat and simmer, stirring occasionally, for 15–20 minutes, until thickened.

2. Preheat the broiler or barbecue. Brush the lamb steaks with oil and cook under the preheated broiler or on the barbecue for 3–5 minutes on each side, depending on how well done you like them. Transfer to serving plates and pour over the sauce. Garnish with basil and serve immediately.

Serves 6

6 lamb steaks
olive oil, for brushing
chopped fresh basil, to garnish

Sweet & spicy tomato sauce
2 tbsp butter
2 tbsp olive oil
2 shallots, finely chopped
2 garlic cloves, finely chopped
1 celery stalk, finely chopped
1 red bell pepper, seeded and chopped
1 lb 2 oz/500 g plum tomatoes, peeled, cored, and chopped
2 tbsp tomato paste
2 tbsp Dijon mustard
1 tbsp honey
2 tbsp brown sugar
1 tbsp chile flakes
1 tbsp cayenne pepper
1 tbsp paprika
scant ½ cup water
salt and pepper

Easy Chicken Curry

1. Melt the butter with half the oil in a pan. Add the onion, garlic, ginger, chile, and celery and cook over low heat, stirring occasionally, for 5 minutes, until softened. Stir in the tomatoes, tomato paste, sugar to taste, spices, and water and season to taste with salt and pepper. Increase the heat to medium and bring to a boil, then reduce the heat and simmer, stirring occasionally, for 15–20 minutes, until thickened.

2. Meanwhile, heat the remaining oil in a skillet. Add the chicken and cook over medium heat, stirring frequently, for 5–7 minutes, until lightly browned all over. Remove with a slotted spoon.

3. Stir the chicken and cream into the sauce and simmer for 6 minutes, until the meat is tender and cooked through. Add the spinach and cook, stirring constantly, for 2–4 minutes, until wilted. Bring back to a boil, then transfer to a warmed serving dish. Serve immediately with naan.

Serves 4

- 2 tbsp butter
- 4 tbsp olive oil
- 1 onion, finely chopped
- 2 garlic cloves, finely chopped
- 1 tbsp chopped fresh ginger
- 1 fresh green chile, seeded and chopped
- 1 celery stalk, finely chopped
- 14 oz/400 g canned chopped tomatoes
- 2 tbsp tomato paste
- brown sugar, to taste
- ½ tsp ground cumin
- ½ tsp ground coriander
- ½ tsp ground turmeric
- ¼ tsp garam masala
- scant ½ cup water
- 1 lb 5 oz/600 g diced chicken
- ⅔ cup heavy cream
- 2⅓ cups baby spinach
- salt and pepper
- warm naan, to serve

51

Chicken with Tomato & Cinnamon Sauce

1. Melt the butter with the oil in a flameproof casserole. Season the chicken well with salt and pepper, add to the casserole, and cook over medium heat, turning frequently, for 8–10 minutes, until evenly browned. Remove from the casserole and set aside.

2. Add the onion, garlic, and celery to the casserole and cook over low heat, stirring occasionally, for 5 minutes, until softened. Stir in the tomatoes, tomato paste, mustard, sugar to taste, lemon juice, stock, oregano, and cinnamon and season to taste with salt and pepper. Increase the heat to medium and bring to a boil, then reduce the heat and simmer, stirring occasionally, for 15 minutes.

3. Return the chicken to the casserole and spoon the sauce over it. Cover and simmer, stirring occasionally, for 30 minutes, until the chicken is tender and cooked through. Serve immediately.

Serves 4

* 4 tbsp butter
* 2 tbsp olive oil
  4 chicken quarters
* 1 onion, finely chopped
* 2 garlic cloves, finely chopped
* 1 celery stalk, finely chopped
* 14 oz/400 g canned chopped tomatoes
* 2 tbsp tomato paste
  1 tsp Dijon mustard
* brown sugar, to taste
  2 tbsp lemon juice
  3 tbsp chicken stock
* 1 tsp dried oregano
  ¾ tsp ground cinnamon
* salt and pepper

Deviled Chicken

1. Put the chicken, carrots, celery, peppercorns, bouquet garni, and salt into a large pan and pour in enough water to cover. Bring to a boil over high heat, then reduce the heat, cover, and simmer for 1½ hours, until tender and cooked through. Remove from the heat and let cool.

2. Meanwhile, make the sauce. Melt the butter with the oil in a pan. Add the shallots, garlic, and celery and cook over low heat, stirring occasionally, for 5 minutes, until softened. Stir in the tomatoes, tomato paste, sugar to taste, Worcestershire sauce, lemon juice, vinegar, and bay leaf and season to taste with salt and pepper. Increase the heat to medium and bring to a boil, then reduce the heat and simmer, stirring occasionally, for 15–20 minutes, until thickened.

3. Preheat the broiler. Remove the chicken from the pan and strain the cooking liquid into a bowl. Remove and discard the skin, cut the chicken into 8 pieces, and put them into a flameproof casserole. Brush the chicken pieces with the melted butter and cook under the preheated broiler for 8 minutes on each side, until evenly browned.

4. Remove and discard the bay leaf from the sauce and stir in 1¼ cups of the reserved cooking liquid. Pour the sauce over the chicken pieces and cook over medium heat for 10–15 minutes, until cooked through. Garnish with thyme and serve immediately.

Serves 4

1 chicken, weighing 5 lb/2.25 kg
2 carrots, cut into chunks
1 celery stalk, cut into short lengths
6 black peppercorns
1 bouquet garni
pinch of salt
2 tbsp melted butter
fresh thyme leaves, to garnish

Devil sauce
2 tbsp butter
2 tbsp olive oil
2 shallots, finely chopped
2 garlic cloves, finely chopped
1 celery stalk, finely chopped
14 oz/400 g canned chopped tomatoes
2 tbsp tomato paste
brown sugar, to taste
3 tbsp Worcestershire sauce
1 tbsp lemon juice
2 tbsp tarragon vinegar
1 bay leaf
salt and pepper

Cajun Chicken

1. Heat the oil in a flameproof casserole. Add the chicken and cook over medium heat, for 3–5 minutes on each side, until evenly browned. Remove and set aside.

2. Reduce the heat to low, stir in half the flour, and cook, stirring constantly, for 1 minute, then stir in the remaining flour. Cook, stirring constantly, until the mixture is the color of peanut butter. Immediately add the onion, garlic, celery, and bell pepper and cook, stirring constantly, for 4 minutes. Add the oregano, thyme, bay leaf, and chiles and cook, stirring, for an additional minute, then remove the casserole from the heat and stir in the tomatoes, tomato paste, and sugar to taste. Season to taste with salt and pepper.

3. Return the casserole to the heat and gradually stir in the stock. Bring to a boil, stirring constantly, then return the chicken to the casserole. Reduce the heat, cover, and simmer, stirring occasionally, for 45 minutes, until the chicken is tender and cooked through. If the sauce seems too runny, remove the lid for the final 15 minutes of the cooking time.

4. Remove and discard the bay leaf. Taste and adjust the seasoning, adding salt and pepper if needed, and stir in the Tabasco, if using. Serve immediately.

Serves 4

* 5 tbsp olive oil
* 4 skinless, boneless chicken breasts, about 6 oz/175 g each
* ½ cup all-purpose flour
* 1 onion, finely chopped
* 2 garlic cloves, finely chopped
* 1 celery stalk, finely chopped
* 1 green bell pepper, seeded and chopped
* ½ tsp dried oregano
* ½ tsp dried thyme
* 1 bay leaf
* 2 fresh red chiles, seeded and chopped
* 14 oz/400 g canned chopped tomatoes
* 2 tbsp tomato paste
* brown sugar, to taste
* 1¼ cups chicken stock
* dash of Tabasco sauce (optional)
* salt and pepper

54

Chicken & Spicy Tomato Sauce Parcels

1. First, make the sauce. Melt the butter with the oil in a pan. Add the onion, garlic, celery, and bell peppers and cook over low heat, stirring occasionally, for 5 minutes, until softened. Stir in the tomatoes, sun-dried tomato paste, sugar to taste, paprika, chili powder, thyme, and water and season to taste with salt and pepper. Increase the heat to medium and bring to a boil, then reduce the heat and simmer, stirring occasionally, for 15–20 minutes, until thickened.

2. Meanwhile, preheat the oven to 375°F/190°C. Cut 4 squares of wax paper, each large enough to enclose a chicken breast. Put 1 chicken breast on each square.

3. Divide the sauce among the chicken breasts and top each with a tarragon sprig. Fold the paper over fairly loosely and double fold the edges to seal. Put the parcels on a baking sheet and bake in the preheated oven for 35–40 minutes, until the chicken is cooked through and tender. Serve immediately.

Serves 4

4 skinless, boneless chicken breasts, about 6 oz/175 each

4 fresh tarragon sprigs

Spicy tomato sauce
- 2 tbsp butter
- 2 tbsp olive oil
- 1 onion, finely chopped
- 2 garlic cloves, finely chopped
- 1 celery stalk, finely chopped
- 2 orange bell peppers, seeded and chopped
- 14 oz/400 g canned chopped tomatoes
- 2 tbsp sun-dried tomato paste
- brown sugar, to taste
- 1 tbsp paprika
- 1 tsp chili powder
- 1 tsp dried thyme
- scant ½ cup water
- salt and pepper

55

Red Snapper in Hot Pepper & Tomato Sauce

1. First, make the sauce. Heat the oil in a pan, then add the onion, garlic, celery, and chile and cook over low heat, stirring occasionally, for 5 minutes, until softened. Stir in the pimientos, tomatoes, tomato paste, sugar to taste, cilantro, olives, and water and season to taste with salt and pepper. Increase the heat to medium and bring to a boil, then reduce the heat and simmer, stirring occasionally, for 15–20 minutes, until thickened.

2. Meanwhile, preheat the oven to 350°F/180°C. Combine the flour, chili powder, salt, and pepper in a plastic bag. Add the fish fillets, a few at a time, hold the top closed, and shake gently to coat. Heat the oil in a skillet, then add the fish, in batches, and cook for 5 minutes on each side, until golden brown. Transfer the fish to a large ovenproof dish and set aside.

3. Halve the eggs, remove the yolks, and chop. (You do not need the egg whites.)

4. Pour the sauce over the fish and bake in the preheated oven for 10–15 minutes, until the flesh flakes easily. Sprinkle with the chopped egg yolks. Garnish with cilantro and serve immediately.

Serves 4

½ cup all-purpose flour
1 tsp chili powder
1 tsp salt
1 tsp pepper
2 lb/900 g red snapper fillets
3 tbsp olive oil
2 hard-cooked eggs

Hot pepper & tomato sauce
* 2 tbsp olive oil
* 1 onion, finely chopped
* 2 garlic cloves, finely chopped
* 1 celery stalk, finely chopped
  1 fresh red chile, finely chopped
  4–6 canned pimientos, drained and finely chopped
* 14 oz/400 g canned chopped tomatoes
* 2 tbsp tomato paste
* brown sugar, to taste
* 1 tbsp chopped fresh cilantro, plus extra to garnish
  ½ cup sliced pimiento-stuffed olives
* scant ½ cup water
* salt and pepper

56

Fish with Indian Tomato Sauce

① Combine 1 teaspoon of salt and 1½ teaspoons of the turmeric in a small bowl. Gently rub the mixture all over the fish cubes. Heat the oil in a deep skillet. Add the fish cubes and cook over medium heat, turning frequently, for 5 minutes, until golden brown. Remove with a slotted spoon and set aside.

② Reduce the heat, add the onions, and cook, stirring occasionally, for 8–10 minutes, until golden brown. Stir in the garlic, sugar, coriander, chile flakes, garam masala, and the remaining turmeric and cook, stirring constantly, for 2 minutes. Add the tomatoes, tomato paste, sour cream, lime juice, and chiles, increase the heat, and bring to a boil. Reduce the heat and simmer, stirring occasionally, for 15 minutes, until thickened.

③ Return the fish cubes to the pan and simmer, stirring occasionally, for 10 minutes. Taste and adjust the seasoning, adding salt and pepper if needed. Transfer to a warmed serving dish and serve immediately.

Serves 4

2 tsp ground turmeric

2 lb 4 oz/1 kg monkfish fillet, cut into 1½-inch/4-cm cubes

4 tbsp peanut oil

2 onions, thinly sliced

2 garlic cloves, finely chopped

1 tsp brown sugar

1 tbsp ground coriander

1 tsp chile flakes

2 tsp garam masala

1 lb 2 oz/500 g plum tomatoes, peeled, cored, and finely chopped

2 tbsp tomato paste

2 tbsp sour cream

1 tbsp lime juice

4 fresh green chiles, slit in half lengthwise and seeded

salt and pepper

57

Monkfish & Shrimp Kabobs with Romesco Sauce

1. First, make the sauce. Melt the butter with half the oil in a pan. Add the onion, garlic, and celery and cook over low heat, stirring occasionally, for 5 minutes, until softened. Stir in the pimiento, tomatoes, tomato paste, chile flakes, sugar to taste, stock, and sherry and season to taste with salt and pepper. Increase the heat to medium and bring to a boil, then reduce the heat and simmer, stirring occasionally, for 30 minutes, until thickened.

2. Meanwhile, preheat the broiler. Spread out the almonds on a baking sheet and toast under the broiler, turning occasionally, for a few minutes, until golden. Transfer to a food processor or blender and grind coarsely. Add the remaining oil and the vinegar and process until combined.

3. When the sauce has thickened, add to the almond mixture, a little at a time, and process until smooth. Taste and adjust the seasoning, adding salt and pepper if needed. Transfer to a clean pan and keep warm over very low heat.

4. Preheat the broiler or barbecue. Brush 6 metal skewers with oil. Thread the monkfish cubes and shrimp alternately onto the skewers and brush with oil. Cook under the preheated broiler or on the barbecue, turning occasionally, for 6–8 minutes, until the fish flakes easily and the shrimp have turned pink. Transfer the skewers to a large serving plate and spoon the sauce into a serving bowl. Serve immediately.

Serves 6

olive oil, for brushing

1 lb 2 oz/500 g monkfish fillet, cut into 1-inch/2.5-cm cubes

24 jumbo shrimp, peeled and deveined

Romesco sauce
- 2 tbsp butter
- 2 tbsp olive oil
- 1 onion, finely chopped
- 3 garlic cloves, finely chopped
- 1 celery stalk, finely chopped
- 1 canned pimiento, drained and chopped
- 1 lb 2 oz/500 g plum tomatoes, peeled, cored, and chopped
- 2 tbsp tomato paste
- ½ tsp chile flakes
- brown sugar, to taste
- 5 tbsp fish stock
- 2 tbsp dry sherry
- 12 blanched almonds
- 1 tbsp sherry vinegar or red wine vinegar
- salt and pepper

West African Spicy Shrimp

1. First, make the sauce. Melt the butter with the oil in a pan. Add the onion and garlic and cook over low heat, stirring occasionally, for 5 minutes, until softened. Stir in the tomatoes, tomato paste, sugar to taste, oregano, bay leaf, and water and season to taste with salt and pepper. Increase the heat to medium and bring to a boil, then reduce the heat and simmer, stirring occasionally, for 20–25 minutes, until thickened.

2. Meanwhile, heat the oil in a large skillet. Add the onions and garlic and cook over low heat, stirring occasionally, for 5 minutes, until softened. Add the shrimp and cook, stirring constantly, for 5 minutes, then add the ham and cook, stirring constantly, for an additional 5 minutes.

3. Stir the thyme, basil, and cayenne pepper into the shrimp mixture, add the bay leaf, and season to taste with salt and pepper. Remove the sauce from the heat, then remove and discard the bay leaf and strain the sauce into the pan, pressing down with the back of a spoon. Simmer, stirring frequently, for 15 minutes. Remove and discard the bay leaf. Transfer to a warmed serving dish and serve immediately.

Serves 4

½ cup olive oil

2 onions, finely chopped

1 garlic clove, finely chopped

12 oz/350 g shrimp, peeled and deveined

1⅓ cups diced ham

1 tsp chopped fresh thyme

1 tsp chopped fresh basil

½ tsp cayenne pepper

1 bay leaf

salt and pepper

Tomato sauce

✳ 2 tbsp butter

✳ 2 tbsp olive oil

✳ 1 small onion, finely chopped

✳ 2 garlic cloves, finely chopped

✳ 1 lb 2 oz/500 g plum tomatoes, peeled, cored, and chopped

✳ 2 tbsp tomato paste

✳ brown sugar, to taste

✳ 1 tsp dried oregano

✳ 1 bay leaf

✳ scant ½ cup water

✳ salt and pepper

Roast Potato Wedges with Tomato & Chile Dipping Sauce

1. First, make the sauce. Melt the butter with the oil in a pan. Add the onion, garlic, and celery and cook over low heat, stirring occasionally, for 5 minutes, until softened. Stir in the tomatoes, tomato paste, chiles, vinegar, sugar to taste, and water and season to taste with salt and pepper. Increase the heat to medium and bring to a boil, then reduce the heat and simmer, stirring occasionally, for 20–30 minutes, until thickened.

2. Meanwhile, preheat the oven to 475°F/240°C. Brush a roasting pan with 2 tablespoons of the oil and put it in the oven to heat. Cut the potatoes in half and then into wedges. Brush the potato wedges with the remaining oil.

3. Remove the roasting pan from the oven and spread out the potato wedges in a single layer in the bottom. Sprinkle with the paprika and sea salt to taste. Roast in the preheated oven, turning occasionally, for 20–30 minutes, until golden brown and crisp all over.

4. Stir the cilantro into the sauce and spoon into a serving bowl. Transfer the potato wedges to a warmed serving dish and serve immediately with the sauce for dipping.

Serves 4

⅔ cup olive oil
4 baking potatoes
1 tbsp sweet paprika
sea salt

Tomato & chile dipping sauce
* 2 tbsp butter
* 2 tbsp olive oil
* 1 onion, finely chopped
* 2 garlic cloves, finely chopped
* 1 celery stalk, finely chopped
* 14 oz/400 g canned chopped tomatoes
* 2 tbsp tomato paste
* 2–3 fresh red chiles, seeded and finely chopped
* 2 tbsp red wine vinegar
* brown sugar, to taste
* scant ½ cup water
* 1 tbsp chopped fresh cilantro
* salt and pepper

60

Crispy Cheese Puffs with Hot Tomato Dip

1. Sift the flour onto a sheet of wax paper. Pour the olive oil and water into a pan and bring to a boil over low heat. As soon as the mixture boils, remove the pan from the heat and tip in the flour all at once, then beat well with a wooden spoon until the mixture is smooth and comes away from the side of the pan. Let cool for a few minutes, then gradually beat in the beaten egg, a little at a time. Stir in the cheese and paprika and set aside in the refrigerator.

2. To make the hot tomato dip, melt the butter with the olive oil in a pan. Add the onion, garlic, and celery and cook over low heat, stirring occasionally, for 5 minutes, until softened. Stir in the tomatoes, tomato paste, cumin, coriander, and cardamom seeds and season to taste with salt and pepper. Increase the heat to medium and bring to a boil, then reduce the heat and simmer, stirring occasionally, for 25–30 minutes, until thickened. Press through a strainer into a clean pan and stir in the sugar, vinegar, chile flakes, and Worcestershire sauce. Bring the mixture to a boil, then reduce the heat and simmer, stirring occasionally.

3. Meanwhile, heat enough peanut oil for deep-frying in a deep-fat fryer to 350–375°F/180–190°C, or until a cube of bread browns in 30 seconds. Drop teaspoonfuls of the cheese mixture into the hot oil, in batches, and fry for 2–3 minutes, until puffed up, crispy, and golden brown. Drain on paper towels. Serve immediately with the hot tomato dip.

Serves 6

generous ½ cup all-purpose flour
¼ cup olive oil
⅔ cup water
2 eggs, lightly beaten
½ cup grated cheddar cheese
½ tsp paprika
peanut oil, for deep-frying

Hot tomato dip
* 2 tbsp butter
* 2 tbsp olive oil
* 1 onion, thinly sliced
* 2 garlic cloves, finely chopped
* 1 celery stalk, finely chopped
* 2 lb 4 oz/1 kg plum tomatoes, peeled, cored, and chopped
* 2 tbsp tomato paste
1 tsp ground cumin
1 tsp ground coriander
1 tsp cardamom seeds
* 1 tsp brown sugar
1 tbsp white wine vinegar
pinch of chile flakes
dash of Worcestershire sauce
* salt and pepper

61

Zucchini Fritters with Peppery Tomato Sauce

1. First, make the sauce. Melt the butter with the oil in a pan. Add the shallots, garlic, celery, and cloves and cook over low heat, stirring occasionally, for 5 minutes, until softened. Remove and discard the garlic and cloves. Add the breadcrumbs and cook, stirring frequently, for 3 minutes. Stir in the tomatoes, tomato paste, sugar to taste, and water. Increase the heat to medium and bring to a boil, then reduce the heat and simmer, stirring occasionally, for 30 minutes, until thickened.

2. Meanwhile, coarsely grate the zucchini onto a clean dish towel, then gather up the sides and squeeze tightly to remove the excess moisture. Transfer the zucchini to a bowl, stir in the Parmesan, eggs, and flour, and season to taste with salt and pepper.

3. Pour the peanut oil into a large skillet to a depth of ¾ inch/ 2 cm and heat. Add 3 heaps of the zucchini mixture, each 2 tablespoonfuls, flatten slightly, and cook for 2–3 minutes on each side. Remove and drain on paper towels. Keep warm while you cook more fritters in the same way until all the mixture has been used.

4. Transfer the fritters to a warmed serving plate. Remove the sauce from the heat and season lightly with salt and generously with pepper. Transfer to a warmed serving bowl and serve immediately with the fritters.

Serves 4–6

1 lb 2 oz/500 g zucchini
⅔ cup grated Parmesan cheese
2 eggs, lightly beaten
4 tbsp all-purpose flour
peanut oil, for deep-frying
salt and pepper

Peppery tomato sauce
* 2 tbsp butter
* 2 tbsp olive oil
2 shallots, finely chopped
* 2 garlic cloves
* 1 celery stalk, finely chopped
2 cloves
3 tbsp dry breadcrumbs
* 14 oz/400 g canned chopped tomatoes
* 2 tbsp tomato paste
* brown sugar, to taste
* scant ½ cup water
* salt and pepper

Comforting

62

Little Spanish Meatballs in Smooth Tomato Sauce

1. First, make the sauce. Melt the butter with the oil in a large flameproof casserole. Add the shallots, garlic, and celery and cook over low heat, stirring occasionally, for 5 minutes, until softened. Stir in the tomatoes, tomato paste, sugar, thyme, bay leaf, and milk and season to taste with salt and pepper. Increase the heat to medium and bring to a boil, then reduce the heat and simmer, stirring frequently, for 30 minutes, until thickened.

2. Meanwhile, using your hands, combine the ground beef, onion, bell pepper, rice, paprika, and egg in a large bowl until thoroughly mixed. Dust your hands with flour and shape pieces of the mixture into balls about 1½ inches/4 cm in diameter. Set aside.

3. Remove the casserole from the heat. Remove and discard the bay leaf, then strain the sauce into a bowl, pressing the vegetables through with the back of a wooden spoon. Return the sauce to the casserole and stir in the cayenne pepper.

4. Add the meatballs to the casserole and bring to a boil over medium heat. Reduce the heat, cover, and simmer for 40–45 minutes, until the meatballs are cooked through. Serve immediately.

Serves 6

1 lb 9 oz/700 g ground beef

1 Bermuda onion, finely chopped

1 red bell pepper, seeded and chopped

scant ½ cup long-grain rice, soaked for 30 minutes and drained

1 tbsp paprika

1 extra large egg, lightly beaten

all-purpose flour, for dusting

Smooth tomato sauce

2 tbsp butter

2 tbsp olive oil

2 shallots, finely chopped

2 garlic cloves, finely chopped

1 celery stalk, finely chopped

14 oz/400 g canned chopped tomatoes

4 tbsp tomato paste

1 tbsp brown sugar

1 tbsp chopped fresh thyme

1 bay leaf

1 cup milk

pinch of cayenne pepper

salt and pepper

Steak with Sweet & Sour Tomato Relish

1. First, make the relish. Melt the butter with the olive oil in a pan. Add the shallot, garlic, and celery and cook over low heat, stirring occasionally, for 5 minutes, until softened. Stir in the tomatoes, tomato paste, sugar, vinegar, ginger, and lime and season to taste with salt and pepper. Increase the heat to medium and bring to a boil, then reduce the heat and simmer, stirring occasionally, for 30 minutes, until thickened. Remove the pan from the heat and transfer the relish to a bowl. Cover with plastic wrap and let cool.

2. Meanwhile, using a sharp knife, cut through each steak horizontally almost completely to make a pocket. Spread 1 teaspoon of the creamed horseradish in each pocket. Rub the steaks with the garlic and season well with salt and pepper. Put them on a plate, cover with plastic wrap, and let stand for 30 minutes.

3. Preheat the broiler. Brush the steaks with sunflower oil and cook under the preheated broiler for 2–3 minutes on each side for medium-rare. If you prefer your steak well done, then reduce the heat and broil for an additional 5–8 minutes on each side. Serve immediately with the relish.

Serves 4

4 sirloin steaks, about
  8 oz/225 g each
4 tsp creamed horseradish
2 garlic cloves, finely chopped
sunflower oil, for brushing
salt and pepper

Sweet & sour tomato relish
1 tbsp butter
1 tbsp olive oil
1 shallot, finely chopped
3 garlic cloves, finely chopped
½ celery stalk, finely chopped
9 oz/250 g red cherry tomatoes
1 tbsp tomato paste
¼ cup brown sugar
¼ cup white wine vinegar
1 piece preserved ginger
  (from a jar), drained and
  chopped
½ lime, thinly sliced
salt and pepper

Cabbage Rolls with Beef in Sweet Tomato Sauce

1. Bring a large pan of water to a boil, add the whole cabbage, and boil for 4 minutes. Drain and let cool slightly, then separate the leaves.

2. Using your hands, combine the ground beef, fresh tomatoes, rice, lemon juice and rind, and parsley in a bowl and season to taste with salt and pepper. Shape the mixture into about 12 small sausage shapes. Wrap each in a cabbage leaf, tucking in the sides, and tie with fine string. Set aside.

3. To make the sauce, melt the butter with the olive oil in a pan. Add the onion, garlic, and celery and cook over low heat, stirring occasionally, for 5 minutes, until softened. Stir in the canned tomatoes, tomato paste, sugar, honey, basil, and water and season to taste with salt and pepper. Increase the heat to medium and bring to a boil, then reduce the heat and simmer, stirring occasionally, for 15–20 minutes, until thickened.

4. Heat the sunflower oil in a large pan. Add the cabbage rolls and cook over medium heat, turning frequently, for a few minutes, until lightly browned. Reduce the heat and pour the sauce over them, then cover and simmer for 1 hour.

5. Using a slotted spoon, remove the cabbage rolls from the pan. Remove and discard the string and transfer the rolls to a serving dish. Pour the sauce over them and serve immediately.

Serves 4

1 head of savoy cabbage, coarse leaves removed

1 lb 2 oz/500 g ground beef

2 tomatoes, peeled and chopped

2 tbsp long-grain rice

juice and grated rind of ½ lemon

1 tbsp chopped fresh parsley

3 tbsp sunflower oil

salt and pepper

Sweet tomato sauce

2 tbsp butter

2 tbsp olive oil

1 onion, finely chopped

2 garlic cloves, finely chopped

1 celery stalk, finely chopped

14 oz/400 g canned chopped tomatoes

2 tbsp tomato paste

1 tbsp brown sugar

1 tbsp honey

1 tbsp chopped fresh basil

scant ½ cup water

salt and pepper

Pork Chops with Tomato & Mushroom Sauce

1. Preheat the broiler to high. Brush the chops with the sunflower oil, sprinkle with the sage, and season well with salt and pepper. Cook under the preheated broiler for 5 minutes on each side, then reduce the heat and broil for an additional 10–15 minutes on each side, until cooked through and tender.

2. Meanwhile, make the sauce. Melt the butter with the olive oil in a pan. Add the shallots, garlic, and celery and cook over low heat, stirring occasionally, for 5 minutes, until softened. Add the mushrooms and cook, stirring occasionally, for an additional 3 minutes. Stir in the tomatoes, tomato paste, sugar to taste, parsley, and water and season to taste with salt and pepper. Increase the heat to medium and bring to a boil, then reduce the heat and simmer, stirring occasionally, for 15–20 minutes, until thickened.

3. Transfer the chops to warmed serving plates. Pour the sauce over them and serve immediately.

Serves 4

4 boneless pork chops
2 tbsp sunflower oil
1 tsp dried sage
salt and pepper

Tomato & mushroom sauce
* 2 tbsp butter
* 2 tbsp olive oil
2 shallots, finely chopped
* 2 garlic cloves, finely chopped
* 1 celery stalk, finely chopped
1¼ cups sliced mushrooms
* 14 oz/400 g canned chopped tomatoes
* 2 tbsp tomato paste
* brown sugar, to taste
* 2 tbsp chopped fresh flat-leaf parsley
* scant ½ cup water
* salt and pepper

Prosciutto & Gorgonzola Parcels with Buttery Tomato Sauce

1. First, make the sauce. Melt 2 tablespoons of the butter in a pan. Add the shallots, garlic, and celery and cook over low heat, stirring occasionally, for 5 minutes, until softened. Stir in the tomatoes, tomato paste, sugar to taste, and wine and season to taste with salt and pepper. Increase the heat to medium and bring to a boil, then reduce the heat and simmer, stirring occasionally, for 15–20 minutes, until thickened.

2. Meanwhile, lay a slice of prosciutto on a board and put a second slice across it to form a cross. Put one-quarter of the cheese in the center, sprinkle with 1 teaspoon of the chives, and add one-quarter of the diced pear. Sprinkle with one-quarter of the walnuts and fold over the sides of the prosciutto to make a parcel. Make 3 more parcels in the same way. Preheat the broiler.

3. Dice the remaining butter. Remove the pan from the heat and beat the sauce well, then beat in the butter, 1 piece at a time, making sure that each piece has been fully incorporated before adding the next. Stir in the chives and basil and reheat gently.

4. Put the prosciutto parcels in the broiler pan and cook under the preheated broiler for 2 minutes on each side, until the cheese is melting and the ham is crispy. Transfer to warmed plates and serve immediately with the sauce.

Serves 4

8 slices prosciutto

4 oz/115 g Gorgonzola cheese, thinly sliced

4 tsp snipped fresh chives

1 pear, peeled, cored, and diced

¼ cup chopped walnuts

Buttery tomato sauce

¾ cup butter

2 shallots, finely chopped

1 garlic clove, finely chopped

1 celery stalk, finely chopped

1 lb 2 oz/500 g plum tomatoes, peeled, cored, and chopped

2 tbsp tomato paste

brown sugar, to taste

scant ½ cup dry white wine

2 tsp snipped fresh chives

1 tbsp chopped fresh basil

salt and pepper

Spaghetti all'Amatriciana

① First, make the sauce. Melt the butter with the oil in a pan. Add the onion, garlic, celery, and carrot and cook over low heat, stirring occasionally, for 5 minutes, until softened. Add the bacon and cook, stirring frequently, for an additional 4 minutes. Pour in the wine and cook until the alcohol has evaporated. Stir in the tomatoes, tomato paste, sugar to taste, and oregano and season to taste with salt and pepper. Increase the heat to medium and bring to a boil, then reduce the heat and simmer, stirring occasionally, for 15–20 minutes, until thickened.

② Meanwhile, bring a large pan of lightly salted water to a boil. Add the spaghetti, bring back to a boil, and cook for 8–10 minutes, until tender but still firm to the bite. Drain and turn into a warmed serving dish.

③ Add the sauce to the spaghetti and toss well to coat. Sprinkle with the cheese, garnish with basil, and serve immediately.

Serves 4–6

1 lb 2 oz/500 g dried spaghetti

1⅓ cups grated Pecorino Romano cheese

salt

chopped fresh basil, to garnish

Amatriciana sauce

✳ 2 tbsp butter

✳ 2 tbsp olive oil

✳ 1 large onion, finely chopped

✳ 2 garlic cloves, finely chopped

✳ 1 celery stalk, finely chopped

1 carrot, finely chopped

7 slices bacon, chopped

scant ½ cup dry white wine

✳ 14 oz/400 g canned chopped tomatoes

✳ 2 tbsp tomato paste

✳ brown sugar, to taste

✳ ½ tsp dried oregano

✳ salt and pepper

One-Pot Lamb in Rich Red Sauce

1. Cook the lamb chops in a large skillet without any added fat over medium heat for 2–3 minutes on each side, until lightly browned. Remove the skillet from the heat and transfer the chops to a plate.

2. Wipe out the skillet with paper towels and return to the heat. Melt the butter with the oil in the skillet. Add the onion, garlic, celery, and bell peppers and cook over low heat, stirring occasionally, for 5 minutes, until softened. Stir in the tomatoes, tomato paste, sugar to taste, basil, and water and season to taste with salt and pepper. Increase the heat to medium and bring to a boil.

3. Return the chops to the pan, spooning the sauce over them. Reduce the heat and simmer, stirring occasionally, for 15–20 minutes, until the sauce has thickened and the lamb is tender. Stir in the olives, then taste and adjust the seasoning, adding salt and pepper if needed. Garnish with basil and serve immediately.

Serves 4

12 lamb rib chops, trimmed of excess fat

✳ 2 tbsp butter

✳ 2 tbsp olive oil

✳ 1 onion, finely chopped

✳ 2 garlic cloves, finely chopped

✳ 1 celery stalk, finely chopped

2 red bell peppers, seeded and sliced

✳ 14 oz/400 g canned chopped tomatoes

✳ 2 tbsp tomato paste

✳ brown sugar, to taste

✳ 2 tbsp chopped fresh basil, plus extra to garnish

✳ scant ½ cup water

2 tbsp chopped pitted black olives

✳ salt and pepper

Lamb Hash with Mushrooms & Tomato Sauce

1. First, make the sauce. Melt the butter with the oil in a pan. Add the onion, garlic, and celery and cook over low heat, stirring occasionally, for 5 minutes, until softened. Stir in the tomatoes, tomato paste, sugar to taste, basil, oregano, and water and season to taste with salt and pepper. Increase the heat to medium and bring to a boil, then reduce the heat and simmer, stirring occasionally, for 15–20 minutes, until thickened.

2. Preheat the oven to 350°F/180°C. Melt 2 tablespoons of the butter in a large pan. Add the mushrooms and cook over medium heat, stirring frequently, for 5 minutes, until softened. Stir in the flour and cook, stirring constantly, for 1 minute, then remove the pan from the heat. Gradually stir in the stock, a little at a time, then return the pan to the heat and cook, stirring constantly, for 3–4 minutes, until thick and smooth. Remove the pan from the heat and stir in the sherry, parsley, and lamb. Transfer to a large ovenproof dish and set aside.

3. Pour the sauce over the lamb mixture. Combine the cheese and breadcrumbs in a small bowl and sprinkle over the top. Dot with the remaining butter and bake in the preheated oven for 30 minutes, until the topping is golden and crisp. Serve immediately.

Serves 4

3 tbsp butter
3¼ cups chopped mushrooms
1 tbsp all-purpose flour
1¼ cups chicken stock
1 tbsp dry sherry
1 tbsp chopped fresh parsley
3½ cups chopped cooked lamb
½ cup grated cheddar cheese
½ cup fresh breadcrumbs

Tomato sauce
* 2 tbsp butter
* 2 tbsp olive oil
* 1 onion, finely chopped
* 2 garlic cloves, finely chopped
* 1 celery stalk, finely chopped
* 14 oz/400 g canned chopped tomatoes
* 2 tbsp tomato paste
* brown sugar, to taste
* 1 tbsp chopped fresh basil
* 1 tsp dried oregano
* scant ½ cup water
* salt and pepper

Fried Chicken with Tomato & Bacon Sauce

1. First, make the sauce. Melt the butter with the oil in a large pan. Add the onion, garlic, celery, and bacon and cook over low heat, stirring occasionally, for 5 minutes, until softened. Stir in the tomatoes, tomato paste, sugar to taste, and water and season to taste with salt and pepper. Increase the heat to medium and bring to a boil, then reduce the heat and simmer, stirring occasionally, for 15–20 minutes, until thickened.

2. Meanwhile, melt the butter with the oil in a large skillet. Add the chicken and cook over medium–high heat for 4–5 minutes on each side, until evenly browned.

3. Stir the basil and parsley into the sauce. Add the chicken and spoon the sauce over it. Cover and simmer for 10–15 minutes, until cooked through and tender. Garnish with parsley and serve immediately.

Serves 4

2 tbsp butter

2 tbsp olive oil

4 skinless, boneless chicken breasts or 8 skinless, boneless chicken thighs

Tomato & bacon sauce

2 tbsp butter

2 tbsp olive oil

1 large onion, finely chopped

2 garlic cloves, finely chopped

1 celery stalk, finely chopped

4 slices bacon, chopped

14 oz/400 g canned chopped tomatoes

2 tbsp tomato paste

brown sugar, to taste

scant ½ cup water

1 tbsp chopped fresh basil

1 tbsp chopped fresh parsley, plus extra to garnish

salt and pepper

Chicken with Tomato Sauce & Melted Mozzarella

1. First, make the sauce. Melt the butter with the oil in a pan. Add the onion, garlic, and celery and cook over low heat, stirring occasionally, for 5 minutes, until softened. Stir in the tomatoes, tomato paste, sugar to taste, oregano, and water and season to taste with salt and pepper. Increase the heat to medium and bring to a boil, then reduce the heat and simmer, stirring occasionally, for 15–20 minutes, until thickened.

2. Meanwhile, fry the bacon without any additional fat in a large skillet over medium heat for 5 minutes. Remove with tongs and drain on paper towels. Add the butter to the skillet and, when it has melted, stir in the tarragon, add the chicken, and cook, turning occasionally, for 15–20 minutes, until cooked through and tender.

3. Preheat the broiler. Transfer the chicken breasts to a flameproof dish and put a bacon slice on top of each. Pour the tomato sauce over them, cover with the mozzarella slices, and cook under the preheated broiler for 4–5 minutes, until the cheese has melted and is lightly browned. Serve immediately.

Serves 6

6 slices bacon

2 tbsp butter

2 tsp chopped fresh tarragon

6 skinless, boneless chicken breasts, about 6 oz/175 g each

4 oz/115 g mozzarella cheese, sliced

Tomato sauce
- 2 tbsp butter
- 2 tbsp olive oil
- 1 onion, finely chopped
- 2 garlic cloves, finely chopped
- 1 celery stalk, finely chopped
- 14 oz/400 g canned chopped tomatoes
- 2 tbsp tomato paste
- brown sugar, to taste
- 1 tsp dried oregano
- scant ½ cup water
- salt and pepper

72

Salmon & Potatoes with Tomato Sauce Topping

1. First, make the sauce. Melt the butter with the oil in a pan. Add the onions, garlic, and celery and cook over low heat, stirring occasionally, for 5 minutes, until softened. Stir in the tomatoes, tomato paste, sugar to taste, marjoram, and wine and season to taste with salt and pepper. Increase the heat to medium and bring to a boil, then reduce the heat and simmer, stirring occasionally, for 15–20 minutes, until thickened.

2. Meanwhile, preheat the oven to 400°F/200°C. Brush an ovenproof dish with oil. Cook the potatoes in a pan of salted boiling water for 15–20 minutes, until tender but not falling apart. Drain well and cut into thick slices. Gently toss the slices in the oil and put them around the side of the prepared dish. Put the fish in the center.

3. Spoon half the sauce evenly over the fish. Stir the breadcrumbs and cheese into the remainder and spoon it over the fish. Bake in the preheated oven for 15–20 minutes, until the fish flakes easily. Garnish with parsley and serve immediately.

Serves 4

12 new potatoes
1 tbsp olive oil, plus extra for brushing
4 salmon fillets
1½ cups fresh breadcrumbs
⅔ cup grated Parmesan cheese
salt
chopped fresh flat-leaf parsley, to garnish

Tomato sauce
* 2 tbsp butter
* 2 tbsp olive oil
* 2 onions, finely chopped
* 2 garlic cloves, finely chopped
* 1 celery stalk, finely chopped
* 14 oz/400 g canned chopped tomatoes
* 2 tbsp tomato paste
* brown sugar, to taste
* 1 tbsp chopped fresh marjoram
scant ½ cup dry white wine
* salt and pepper

Fish with Tomato, Garlic & Olive Sauce

1. First, make the sauce. Melt the butter with the oil in a pan. Add the onions, garlic, celery, and bell peppers and cook over low heat, stirring occasionally, for 5 minutes, until softened. Stir in the tomatoes, tomato paste, sugar to taste, olives, and water and season to taste with salt and pepper. Increase the heat to medium and bring to a boil, then reduce the heat and simmer, stirring occasionally, for 30 minutes, until thickened.

2. Meanwhile, preheat the oven to 450°F/230°C. Grease a large ovenproof dish with butter. Combine the breadcrumbs, parsley, and lemon rind in a shallow dish. Beat the egg with the milk in a separate shallow dish. Dip the fish fillets, 1 at a time, in the egg mixture and then in the breadcrumb mixture, and put into the prepared dish in a single layer. Melt the butter and drizzle a little of it over the fish. Bake in the preheated oven, drizzling frequently with the remaining melted butter, for 15 minutes, until the flesh flakes easily.

3. Remove the fish from the oven and carefully transfer to a warmed serving dish. Spoon the sauce over the top and serve immediately.

Serves 4

1⅔ cups dry breadcrumbs
2 tbsp chopped fresh parsley
finely grated rind of 1 lemon
1 egg
4 tbsp milk
8–12 flounder or sole fillets
4 tbsp butter, plus extra for greasing

Tomato, garlic & olive sauce

2 tbsp butter
2 tbsp olive oil
2 onions, thinly sliced
2 garlic cloves, finely chopped
1 celery stalk, finely chopped
1 green bell pepper and 1 red bell pepper, seeded and sliced
1 lb 2 oz/500 g tomatoes, peeled, cored, and sliced
2 tbsp tomato paste
brown sugar, to taste
12 pitted kalamata olives
scant ½ cup water
salt and pepper

Monkfish with Tomato, Olive & Caper Sauce

1. First, make the sauce. Melt the butter with the oil in a pan. Add the shallots, garlic, and celery and cook over low heat, stirring occasionally, for 5 minutes, until softened. Stir in the tomatoes, sun-dried tomato paste, sugar to taste, capers, olives, and Pernod and season to taste with salt and pepper. Increase the heat to medium and bring to a boil, then reduce the heat and simmer, stirring occasionally, for 20–25 minutes, until thickened.

2. Meanwhile, put the fish in a large pan in a single layer. Pour in the wine, add the orange rind, peppercorns, and bay leaf and bring just to a boil over medium heat. Reduce the heat so that the water is barely bubbling, cover, and poach for 10–15 minutes, until the flesh flakes easily.

3. Using a spatula, transfer the fish to a warmed serving dish. Strain the cooking liquid into the sauce and bring to a boil. Boil, stirring constantly, for 2–3 minutes, until reduced. Pour the sauce over the fish and serve immediately.

Serves 4

4 monkfish fillets, about 8 oz/225 g each
⅔ cup dry white wine
thinly pared strip of orange rind
6 black peppercorns
1 bay leaf

Tomato, olive & caper sauce
2 tbsp butter
2 tbsp olive oil
2 shallots, finely chopped
2 garlic cloves, finely chopped
1 celery stalk, finely chopped
1 lb 2 oz/500 g plum tomatoes, peeled, cored, and chopped
2 tbsp sun-dried tomato paste
brown sugar, to taste
1 tbsp rinsed capers
½ cup pitted black olives
1 tbsp Pernod
salt and pepper

75

Pissaladière

1. Preheat the oven to 400°F/200°C. Roll out the dough on a lightly floured surface and use to line a 10-inch/25-cm loose-bottom tart pan. Prick the bottom with a fork, line with wax paper, and fill halfway with dried beans. Transfer to a baking sheet and bake in the preheated oven for 10 minutes. Remove the paper and beans, return the tart pan to the oven, and bake for an additional 10 minutes, until lightly colored. Remove from the oven and let cool.

2. Meanwhile, make the sauce. Melt the butter with the oil in a pan. Add the onion, garlic, and celery and cook over low heat, stirring occasionally, for 5 minutes, until softened. Stir in the canned tomatoes, sun-dried tomatoes, tomato paste, sugar to taste, and water and season to taste with salt and pepper. Increase the heat to medium and bring to a boil, then reduce the heat and simmer, stirring occasionally, for 15–20 minutes, until thickened.

3. Remove the pan from the heat and stir in the basil. Spread the sauce evenly over the bottom of the pie shell. Sprinkle with the Parmesan and arrange the anchovies in a lattice pattern on top. Put an olive half in each diamond shape. Drizzle with oil and, if you want to serve the pissaladière piping hot, return to the oven for 10–15 minutes. Alternatively, serve warm or let cool completely.

Serves 4

9 oz/250 g store-bought flaky pie dough, thawed if frozen
all-purpose flour, for dusting
3 tbsp grated Parmesan cheese
1¾ oz/50 g canned anchovy fillets, drained and cut into strips
½ cup halved pitted black olives
olive oil, for drizzling

Tomato sauce
* 2 tbsp butter
* 2 tbsp olive oil
* 1 onion, finely chopped
* 2 garlic cloves, finely chopped
* 1 celery stalk, finely chopped
* 14 oz/400 g canned chopped tomatoes
  2 tbsp sliced drained sun-dried tomatoes in oil
* 2 tbsp tomato paste
* brown sugar, to taste
* scant ½ cup water
* 1 tbsp chopped fresh basil
* salt and pepper

Baked Gnocchi with Tomato Sauce

1. To make the gnocchi, whisk the egg yolks with the granulated sugar in a pan until pale and creamy. Sift the flour, cornstarch, and salt into a bowl, then gradually beat into the egg yolk mixture. Stir in the melted butter and 1 cup of the Parmesan. Set the pan over medium heat and gradually stir in the milk. Cook, stirring constantly, for 3–4 minutes, until thick and smooth. Remove the pan from the heat and turn out the mixture onto a baking sheet rinsed with cold water. Spread out to a thickness of about ½ inch/1 cm and smooth the surface. Chill in the refrigerator for 30 minutes.

2. Meanwhile, make the sauce. Melt the butter with the oil in a pan. Add the onion, garlic, and celery and cook over low heat, stirring occasionally, for 5 minutes, until softened. Stir in the tomatoes, tomato paste, brown sugar to taste, vermouth, parsley, and water and season to taste with salt and pepper. Increase the heat to medium and bring to a boil, then reduce the heat and simmer, stirring occasionally, for 25–30 minutes, until thickened.

3. Meanwhile, preheat the oven to 375°F/190°C. Grease an ovenproof dish with butter. Cut the gnocchi into 1¼–1½-inch/3–4-cm squares and put them into the prepared dish, slightly overlapping. Bake in the preheated oven for 15 minutes. Pour the sauce over the top and bake for an additional 5–10 minutes, until hot. Sprinkle with the remaining Parmesan, garnish with parsley, and serve immediately.

Serves 4

4 egg yolks

2 tsp granulated sugar

½ cup all-purpose flour

2 tbsp cornstarch

pinch of salt

4 tbsp melted butter, plus extra for greasing

1⅓ cups grated Parmesan cheese

scant 2 cups milk

Tomato sauce

- 2 tbsp butter
- 2 tbsp olive oil
- 1 onion, finely chopped
- 2 garlic cloves, finely chopped
- 1 celery stalk, finely chopped
- 1 lb 12 oz/800 g canned chopped tomatoes
- 2 tbsp tomato paste
- brown sugar, to taste
- 1 tbsp dry vermouth
- 1 tbsp chopped fresh flat-leaf parsley, plus extra to garnish
- 5 tbsp water
- salt and pepper

Cheese-Stuffed Onions with Tomato Sauce

1. Preheat the oven to 400°F/200°C. Grease an ovenproof dish, just large enough to hold the onions in a single layer, with butter. Cook the whole peeled onions in a large pan of boiling water for 15 minutes, until tender. Drain and let cool, then carefully scoop out the centers without piercing the shells.

2. Finely chop the scooped-out onion and put it into a bowl with the breadcrumbs and cheese. Season to taste with salt and pepper and mix well. Spoon the mixture into the onion shells, packing it down well and doming the tops. Put the onions into the prepared dish, dot with the butter, and bake in the preheated oven for 20–30 minutes, until golden brown and tender.

3. Meanwhile, make the sauce. Melt the butter with the oil in a pan. Add the scallions, garlic, celery, and carrot and cook over low heat, stirring occasionally, for 5 minutes, until softened. Stir in the tomatoes, tomato paste, sugar to taste, parsley, chives, wine, and Worcestershire sauce and season to taste with salt and pepper. Increase the heat to medium and bring to a boil, then reduce the heat and simmer, stirring occasionally, for 15–20 minutes, until thickened.

4. When the onions are cooked through, transfer them to a warmed serving dish. Spoon the sauce around them and serve immediately.

Serves 4

4 large onions
4 tbsp fresh breadcrumbs
1 cup grated cheddar cheese
2 tbsp butter, plus extra for greasing
salt and pepper

Tomato sauce
1 tbsp butter
1 tbsp olive oil
2 scallions, finely chopped
1 garlic clove, finely chopped
1 small celery stalk, finely chopped
1 small carrot, finely chopped
7 oz/200 g canned chopped tomatoes
1 tbsp tomato paste
brown sugar, to taste
1 tbsp chopped fresh parsley
1 tbsp snipped fresh chives
¼ cup red wine
1 tbsp Worcestershire sauce
salt and pepper

78

Cauliflower Casserole

1. First, make the sauce. Melt the butter with the oil in a pan. Add the onion, garlic, and celery and cook over low heat, stirring occasionally, for 5 minutes, until softened. Stir in the tomatoes, tomato paste, sugar to taste, parsley, and water and season to taste with salt and pepper. Increase the heat to medium and bring to a boil, then reduce the heat and simmer, stirring occasionally, for 15–20 minutes, until thickened.

2. Meanwhile, preheat the oven to 375°F/190°C. Grease a large ovenproof dish with butter. Bring a large pan of salted water to a boil. Add the cauliflower and cook over medium heat for 10–12 minutes, until tender. Drain well and put into the prepared casserole.

3. Spoon the sauce over the cauliflower. Combine the breadcrumbs, Gruyère, and Parmesan in a bowl and sprinkle over the top. Drizzle with the melted butter and bake in the preheated oven for 30 minutes, until the topping is golden brown. Serve immediately.

Serves 4

1 large head of cauliflower, cut into florets

2 tbsp fresh breadcrumbs

2 tbsp grated Gruyère cheese

2 tbsp grated Parmesan cheese

4 tbsp melted butter, plus extra for greasing

salt

Tomato sauce
* 2 tbsp butter
* 2 tbsp olive oil
* 1 onion, finely chopped
* 2 garlic cloves, finely chopped
* 1 celery stalk, finely chopped
* 1 lb 2 oz/500 g plum tomatoes, peeled, cored, and chopped
* 2 tbsp tomato paste
* brown sugar, to taste
* 1–2 tbsp chopped fresh flat-leaf parsley
* scant ½ cup water
* salt and pepper

Baked Cheese & Eggplant Layers

① First, make the sauce. Melt the butter with the oil in a pan. Add the shallot, garlic, and celery and cook over low heat, stirring occasionally, for 5 minutes, until softened. Stir in the tomatoes, tomato paste, sugar to taste, oregano, and water and season to taste with salt and pepper. Increase the heat to medium and bring to a boil, then reduce the heat and simmer, stirring occasionally, for 15–20 minutes, until thickened.

② Meanwhile, preheat the oven to 350°F/180°C. Spread out the flour on a shallow dish and season to taste with salt and pepper. Dip the eggplant slices in the flour to coat and shake off any excess. Heat the oil in a skillet, add the eggplant slices, in batches, and cook for 2 minutes on each side, until lightly browned. Remove and drain on paper towels.

③ Make alternating layers of eggplant slices, mozzarella slices, and tomato sauce in an ovenproof dish. Sprinkle with the Parmesan and bake in the preheated oven for 25 minutes, until the topping is golden and bubbling. Serve immediately.

Serves 6

½ cup all-purpose flour
2 large eggplants, sliced
6 tbsp olive oil
8 oz/225 g mozzarella cheese, thinly sliced
⅔ cup grated Parmesan cheese
salt and pepper

Tomato sauce
* 1 tbsp butter
* 1 tbsp olive oil
1 shallot, finely chopped
* 1 garlic clove, finely chopped
* 1 small celery stalk, finely chopped
* 7 oz/200 g canned chopped tomatoes
* 1 tbsp tomato paste
* brown sugar, to taste
* ½ tsp dried oregano
* 4 tbsp water
* salt and pepper

Hoppin' John

1. Put the black-eyed peas into a large pan and pour in water to cover. Bring to a boil and boil vigorously for 15 minutes, then remove from the heat and drain. Return the peas to the pan and pour in the 5 cups of water. Bring to a boil, then reduce the heat, partially cover the pan, and simmer for 1½ hours.

2. Meanwhile, make the sauce. Melt the butter with the oil in a pan. Add the onion and cook over low heat, stirring occasionally, for 5 minutes, until softened. Stir in the tomatoes, tomato paste, sugar to taste, cayenne pepper, and the scant ½ cup of water and season to taste with salt and pepper. Increase the heat to medium and bring to a boil, then reduce the heat and simmer, stirring occasionally, for 15 minutes, until thickened.

3. Stir the rice into the pan of peas, cover, and simmer for an additional 15 minutes.

4. Stir the sauce into the pea-and-rice mixture, re-cover the pan, and simmer for an additional 15–20 minutes, until the rice and beans are tender. Serve immediately.

Serves 6

1¼ cups dried black-eyed peas, soaked overnight and drained

5 cups water

generous 1 cup long-grain rice

Tomato sauce
* 2 tbsp butter
* 2 tbsp corn oil
* 1 onion, finely chopped
* 14 oz/400 g canned chopped tomatoes
* 2 tbsp tomato paste
* brown sugar, to taste
½ tsp cayenne pepper
* scant ½ cup water
* salt and pepper

81

Spinach Crêpes with Tomato Sauce

① To make the crêpe batter, sift the flour and salt into a bowl and make a well in the center. Add the eggs and melted butter and mix together, gradually incorporating the dry ingredients. Mix the milk and water in a pitcher and gradually beat into the mixture to form a smooth batter.

② Cook the spinach, in just the water clinging to the leaves after washing, for 5–10 minutes, until wilted. Drain well, pressing out as much liquid as possible. Transfer to a food processor or blender and process to a paste. Stir the spinach into the batter, cover with plastic wrap, and let rest in a cool place.

③ Meanwhile, pour the tomato sauce into a large saucepan and place over a low heat. Heat gently until warmed through.

④ Stir the batter. Heat an 8-inch/20-cm skillet over medium heat and brush with a little melted butter. Pour 3–4 tablespoons of the batter into the skillet, then tilt and rotate the skillet to spread the batter evenly over the bottom. Cook for 30–45 seconds, until the crêpe is set and the underside is golden. Shake the skillet to loosen the crêpe, then flip over with a spatula and cook the other side for 30 seconds. Slide onto a plate. Cook more crêpes in the same way, stacking them interleaved with wax paper.

⑤ Roll up or fold the crêpes and put them on a serving dish. Spoon the tomato sauce over them and serve immediately.

Serves 4–6

2 cups all-purpose flour

pinch of salt

4 eggs

4 tbsp melted butter, plus extra for brushing

1 cup milk

scant 1 cup water

1 lb 2 oz/500 g spinach, coarse stalks removed

✳ 1 quantity Basic Tomato Sauce (see page 10)

Special

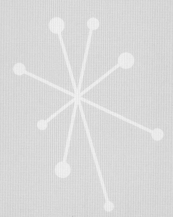

82

Steak Pizzaiola

1. First, make the sauce. Melt the butter with the oil in a pan. Add the onion and garlic and cook over low heat, stirring occasionally, for 5 minutes, until softened. Stir in the tomatoes, tomato paste, sugar to taste, olives, basil, oregano, and water and season to taste with salt and pepper. Increase the heat to medium and bring to a boil, then reduce the heat and simmer, stirring occasionally, for 15–20 minutes, until thickened.

2. Heat the oil in a large skillet. Add the steak and cook over medium heat for 2–3 minutes on each side. Spoon the sauce over each steak and cook for an additional 5 minutes. Serve immediately.

Serves 4

3 tbsp olive oil

4 sirloin steaks, about
   8 oz/225 g each

Pizzaiola sauce
* 2 tbsp butter
* 2 tbsp olive oil
* 1 onion, finely chopped
* 2 garlic cloves, finely chopped
* 1 lb 2 oz/500 g plum tomatoes, peeled, cored, and chopped
* 2 tbsp tomato paste
* brown sugar, to taste
   1 cup chopped pitted green olives
* 1 tbsp chopped fresh basil
* 1 tsp dried oregano
* scant ½ cup water
* salt and pepper

83

Stuffed Veal Rolls in Tomato & Wine Sauce

1. Heat the oil in a large flameproof casserole. Add the sausages and cook over medium heat, turning frequently, for 8–10 minutes, until evenly browned. Transfer to a plate and let cool. Pour off the fat from the casserole.

2. To make the sauce, melt the butter with the oil in the casserole. Add the onion, garlic, and celery and cook over low heat, stirring occasionally, for 5 minutes, until softened. Stir in the tomatoes, tomato paste, sugar to taste, marjoram, and wine and season to taste with salt and pepper. Increase the heat to medium and bring to a boil, then reduce the heat and simmer, stirring occasionally, for 15–20 minutes, until thickened.

3. Meanwhile, preheat the oven to 350°F/180°C. Lay the veal scallops flat on a counter. Put a sausage on the end of each and roll up, then secure with a wooden toothpick. Melt the butter in a skillet. Add the veal rolls and cook over medium heat, turning occasionally, for 6–8 minutes, until evenly browned. Remove the skillet from the heat and transfer the rolls to the casserole.

4. Cover the casserole, transfer to the preheated oven, and bake for 40–45 minutes, until the meat is cooked through and tender. Remove the toothpicks from the rolls and serve immediately.

Serves 4

1 tbsp olive oil
4 Italian cooking sausages, such as luganega
4 veal scallops
4 tbsp butter

Tomato & wine sauce
* 2 tbsp butter
* 2 tbsp olive oil
* 1 onion, finely chopped
* 2 garlic cloves, finely chopped
* 1 celery stalk, finely chopped
* 14 oz/400 g canned chopped tomatoes
* 2 tbsp tomato paste
* brown sugar, to taste
* 1 tbsp chopped fresh marjoram
1¼ cups dry white wine
* salt and pepper

Pork Chops with Creamy Tomato Sauce

1. Preheat the oven to 350°F/180°C. Rub the chops all over with salt, pepper, and two-thirds of the garlic. Melt the butter with the oil in a large flameproof casserole. Add the chops and cook over medium heat for 3–4 minutes on each side, until lightly browned. Remove from the casserole and keep warm.

2. Add the shallots, the remaining garlic, and the celery to the casserole, reduce the heat, and cook, stirring occasionally, for 5 minutes, until softened. Stir in the tomatoes, tomato paste, and sugar to taste and cook, stirring frequently, for 5 minutes. Stir in the mushrooms and sage, season to taste with salt and pepper, and cook, stirring frequently, for an additional 5 minutes.

3. Return the chops to the casserole and pour in the wine and stock. Cover, transfer to the preheated oven, and bake for 30 minutes. Remove the lid, return the casserole to the oven, and bake for an additional 15 minutes, until the meat is tender and cooked through.

4. Transfer the chops to a warmed serving dish and keep warm. Bring the sauce to a boil over medium–high heat and boil for 5–8 minutes, until reduced by half. Remove the casserole from the heat and stir in the cream. Pour the sauce over the chops, garnish with sage, and serve immediately.

Serves 4

4 pork chops
* 3 garlic cloves, finely chopped
* 2 tbsp butter
* 2 tbsp olive oil
  2 shallots, finely chopped
* 1 celery stalk, finely chopped
* 1 lb 2 oz/500 g plum tomatoes, peeled, cored, and chopped
* 2 tbsp tomato paste
* brown sugar, to taste
  3¼ cups thinly sliced mushrooms
* 1 tbsp chopped fresh sage, plus extra to garnish
  ¼ cup white wine
  ¼ cup chicken stock
  ¼ cup heavy cream
* salt and pepper

Pork Chops in Tomato & Green Bell Pepper Sauce

1. Season the chops well with salt and pepper. Melt the butter with the oil in a large skillet. Add the chops and cook over medium heat for 3–4 minutes on each side, until lightly browned. Transfer to a plate and keep warm.

2. Add the onion, garlic, celery, and bell peppers to the skillet, reduce the heat, and cook, stirring occasionally, for 5 minutes, until softened. Stir in the mushrooms and cook, stirring frequently, for an additional 3 minutes. Stir in the tomatoes, tomato paste, sugar to taste, basil, thyme, bay leaf, and wine and season to taste with salt and pepper. Increase the heat to medium and bring to a boil. Return the chops to the skillet, reduce the heat, cover, and simmer, spooning the sauce over the chops frequently, for 40 minutes, until the meat is tender and cooked through.

3. Transfer the chops to a warmed serving dish and keep warm. Mix the cornstarch to a paste with the water in a small bowl, then stir into the skillet. Cook, stirring constantly, for 3–5 minutes, until thickened. Remove and discard the bay leaf and spoon the sauce over the chops. Garnish with parsley and serve immediately.

Serves 4

- 4 pork chops
- 2 tbsp butter
- 2 tbsp olive oil
- 1 onion, finely chopped
- 2 garlic cloves, finely chopped
- 1 celery stalk, finely chopped
- 2 green bell peppers, seeded and finely chopped
- 2½ cups button mushrooms
- 14 oz/400 g canned chopped tomatoes
- 2 tbsp tomato paste
- brown sugar, to taste
- 1 tbsp chopped fresh basil
- ½ tsp chopped fresh thyme
- 1 bay leaf
- scant ½ cup red wine
- 1 tbsp cornstarch
- 2 tbsp water
- salt and pepper
- chopped fresh flat-leaf parsley, to garnish

86

Lamb with Tomato & Eggplant Sauce

(1) First, make the sauce. Melt the butter with the oil in a pan. Add the onion, garlic, and eggplant and cook over low heat, stirring occasionally, for 5 minutes, until softened. Stir in the tomatoes, tomato paste, sugar to taste, parsley, bay leaf, and water and season to taste with salt and pepper. Increase the heat to medium and bring to a boil, then reduce the heat and simmer, stirring occasionally, for 30 minutes, until thickened.

(2) Meanwhile, heat the oil in a skillet. Add the onions and cook over low heat, stirring occasionally, for 5 minutes, until softened. Remove with a slotted spoon and drain on paper towels, then set aside and keep warm.

(3) Return the skillet to the heat and melt the butter. Add the lamb noisettes and cook over medium heat for 4–6 minutes on each side, until tender and cooked to your liking. Transfer to individual serving plates. Remove and discard the bay leaf from the sauce and divide the sauce among the plates. Top the lamb with the reserved fried onions, garnish with parsley, and serve immediately.

Serves 4

1 tbsp olive oil

2 onions, sliced

2 tbsp butter

8 lamb noisettes

Tomato & eggplant sauce

* 2 tbsp butter
* 2 tbsp olive oil
* 1 onion, sliced
* 2 garlic cloves, finely chopped
1 large eggplant, sliced
* 1 lb 2 oz/500 g plum tomatoes, peeled, cored, and chopped
* 2 tbsp tomato paste
* brown sugar, to taste
* 1 tbsp chopped fresh parsley, plus extra to garnish
* 1 bay leaf
* scant ½ cup water
* salt and pepper

87

Lamb Chops in Tomato Sauce with Fava Beans

1. Season the chops well with salt and pepper. Melt the butter with the oil in a large skillet. Add the chops and cook over medium heat for 1–1½ minutes on each side, until evenly browned. Remove the chops from the skillet and set aside.

2. Add the onion, garlic, celery, and bacon to the skillet and cook over low heat, stirring occasionally, for 5 minutes, until the onion has softened. Stir in the tomatoes, tomato paste, sugar to taste, basil, vinegar, and water and season to taste with salt and pepper. Increase the heat to medium and bring to a boil, then reduce the heat and simmer, stirring occasionally, for 10 minutes.

3. Return the chops to the pan and add the fava beans. Partially cover and simmer for 10 minutes, until the lamb is tender and cooked through. Transfer to a warmed serving dish and serve immediately.

Serves 4

8 lamb chops
* 2 tbsp butter
* 2 tbsp olive oil
* 1 onion, finely chopped
* 2 garlic cloves, finely chopped
* 1 celery stalk, finely chopped
2 slices bacon, chopped
* 14 oz/400 g canned chopped tomatoes
* 2 tbsp tomato paste
* brown sugar, to taste
* 2 tbsp chopped fresh basil
1 tbsp red wine vinegar
* scant ½ cup water
scant 2½ cups shelled fresh or frozen fava beans, gray skins removed
* salt and pepper

Spanish Chicken with Tomato & Chocolate Sauce

1. Dust the chicken pieces with flour. Heat the oil in a large skillet. Add the chicken, in batches if necessary, and cook over medium heat, turning occasionally, for 8–10 minutes, until evenly browned. Remove the chicken from the skillet and drain on paper towels. Drain off the fat from the skillet and wipe out with paper towels.

2. To make the sauce, melt the butter with the oil in the same skillet. Add the onion, garlic, and bell pepper and cook over low heat, stirring occasionally, for 5 minutes, until softened. Stir in the tomatoes, tomato paste, sugar to taste, nutmeg, cinnamon, cloves, and wine and season to taste with salt and pepper. Increase the heat to medium and bring to a boil.

3. Return the chicken to the skillet, reduce the heat, cover, and simmer for 20 minutes. Remove the lid from the skillet and simmer for an additional 20 minutes, until the chicken is cooked through and tender and the sauce has thickened. Add the chopped chocolate and stir constantly until it has melted. Garnish with grated chocolate and serve immediately.

Serves 6

6 chicken pieces
all-purpose flour, for dusting
4 tbsp olive oil

Tomato & chocolate sauce
* 2 tbsp butter
* 2 tbsp olive oil
* 1 onion, finely chopped
* 2 garlic cloves, finely chopped
1 red bell pepper, seeded and sliced
* 1 lb 12 oz/800 g canned chopped tomatoes
* 2 tbsp tomato paste
* brown sugar, to taste
½ tsp ground nutmeg
½ tsp ground cinnamon
¼ tsp ground cloves
generous 1 cup dry white wine
2½ oz/70 g bittersweet chocolate, finely chopped, plus extra grated chocolate to garnish
* salt and pepper

Chicken in Tomato & Almond Sauce

1. Melt the butter with the oil in a pan. Add the shallots, garlic, and celery and cook over low heat, stirring occasionally, for 5 minutes, until softened. Remove the pan from the heat and stir in the ground almonds, breadcrumbs, parsley, tomatoes, tomato paste, and sugar to taste and season to taste with salt and pepper. Return the pan to the heat and cook, stirring constantly, for 5 minutes, or until thickened. Remove the pan from the heat.

2. Put the chicken into a large pan. Pour in the hot stock and orange juice, add the bouquet garni and peppercorns, and bring just to a boil. Reduce the heat so that the water is barely simmering, cover, and poach for 20 minutes, until the chicken is cooked through and tender.

3. Transfer the chicken to a warmed serving dish and keep warm. Strain and reserve 5 tablespoons of the cooking liquid, then stir it into the sauce. Return the pan to the heat and cook, stirring constantly, until thoroughly combined and heated through. Pour the sauce over the chicken and sprinkle with the slivered almonds. Garnish with parsley and serve immediately.

Serves 4

- 2 tbsp butter
- 2 tbsp olive oil
- 2 shallots, finely chopped
- 3 garlic cloves, finely chopped
- 1 celery stalk, finely chopped
- ½ cup ground almonds
- 4 tbsp fresh breadcrumbs
- 3 tbsp chopped fresh flat-leaf parsley, plus extra to garnish
- 1 lb 2 oz/500 g plum tomatoes, peeled, cored, and chopped
- 2 tbsp tomato paste
- brown sugar, to taste
- 4 skinless, boneless chicken breasts
- 4 cups hot chicken stock
- juice of ½ orange
- 1 bouquet garni
- 6 black peppercorns
- 2 tbsp slivered almonds
- salt and pepper

Duck with Tomato & Orange Sauce

1. First, make the sauce. Melt the butter with the oil in a pan. Add the shallots, garlic, and celery and cook over low heat, stirring occasionally, for 5 minutes, until softened. Stir in the tomatoes, tomato paste, sugar, stock, orange juice, wine, and vinegar and season to taste with salt and pepper. Increase the heat to medium and bring to a boil, then reduce the heat and simmer, stirring occasionally, for 20–30 minutes, until thickened.

2. Heat a grill pan. Score the skin of the duck breasts through to the flesh. When the grill pan is hot, add the duck breasts, skin-side down, and cook for 8–10 minutes. Turn them over and cook for an additional 4–6 minutes on the other side.

3. Meanwhile, remove the pan of sauce from the heat and let cool slightly. Ladle it into a food processor or blender and process to a paste. Pass the paste through a strainer into a clean pan and heat through gently. If you prefer a thicker sauce, bring to a boil and boil, stirring constantly, until reduced.

4. Divide the sauce among 4 warmed individual plates. Top each with a duck breast, garnish with basil leaves, and serve immediately.

Serves 4

4 duck breasts
fresh basil leaves, to garnish

Tomato & orange sauce
* 2 tbsp butter
* 2 tbsp olive oil
2 shallots, finely chopped
* 1 garlic clove, finely chopped
* 1 celery stalk, finely chopped
* 1 lb 2 oz/500 g plum tomatoes, peeled, cored, and chopped
* 2 tbsp tomato paste
* 1 tsp brown sugar
3 tbsp chicken stock
juice of 2 oranges
2 tbsp dry white wine
1 tsp white wine vinegar
* salt and pepper

91

Halibut in Tomato & Wine Sauce

1. Combine the flour, cilantro, oregano, and ½ teaspoon of each salt and pepper in a shallow dish. Coat the fish fillets in the seasoned flour, shaking off the excess. Melt the butter with the oil in a large skillet. Add the fish and cook over medium heat for 5 minutes on each side, until evenly browned. Remove with a spatula and keep warm.

2. Add the shallots, garlic and celery to the skillet, reduce the heat to low, and cook, stirring occasionally, for 5 minutes, until softened. Stir in the tomatoes, tomato paste, sugar to taste, bay leaf, wine, and vinegar and season to taste with salt and pepper. Increase the heat to medium and bring to a boil. Return the fish to the skillet and add the shrimp. Reduce the heat, cover, and simmer for 10–15 minutes, until the fish flakes easily.

3. Transfer the halibut and shrimp to a warmed serving dish and keep warm. Increase the heat to high and bring the sauce to a boil, stirring constantly. Cook, stirring frequently, for 3–4 minutes, until reduced and thickened. Remove and discard the bay leaf, then pour the sauce over the fish. Serve immediately.

Serves 4

4 tbsp all-purpose flour

1 tbsp finely chopped fresh cilantro

½ tsp dried oregano

4 halibut fillets, about 6 oz/175 g each

2 tbsp butter

2 tbsp olive oil

2 shallots, finely chopped

1 garlic clove, finely chopped

1 celery stalk, finely chopped

2 lb 4 oz/1 kg plum tomatoes, peeled, seeded, and chopped

2 tbsp tomato paste

brown sugar, to taste

1 bay leaf

1¼ cups dry white wine

2 tbsp tarragon vinegar

8 oz/225 g shrimp, peeled and deveined

salt and pepper

92

Sliced Fish in Chinese Tomato Sauce

1. Cut the fish into 1 inch/2.5 cm wide strips. Combine the cornstarch, ground ginger, and salt in a shallow dish, add the pieces of fish, and toss gently. Gently stir in the egg white.

2. Heat the oil in a large skillet. Carefully add the pieces of fish, in batches if necessary, and cook over medium heat, tilting the skillet so that the oil flows around them, for 1 minute. Using a spatula, turn them over and cook for an additional 30 seconds. Remove with the spatula and keep warm. Drain off the oil and wipe the skillet with paper towels, then return to the heat.

3. To make the sauce, melt the butter with the oil in the same skillet. Add the scallions, garlic, and fresh ginger, reduce the heat, and cook, stirring occasionally, for 5 minutes, until softened. Stir in the tomatoes and cook, stirring constantly, for 5 minutes. Stir in the tomato paste, sugar to taste, and soy sauce.

4. Mix together the cornstarch, stock, and rice wine in a bowl until thoroughly combined, then stir into the skillet. Increase the heat to medium and cook, stirring constantly, for a few minutes, until thickened. Return the pieces of fish to the skillet, reduce the heat to low, and simmer for 2–3 minutes, until the fish flakes easily. Transfer the fish and sauce to a warmed serving dish, garnish with scallions, and serve immediately.

Serves 4

1 lb 9 oz/700 g flounder fillets, skinned

2 tbsp cornstarch

½ tsp ground ginger

1 tsp salt

1 extra large egg white, lightly beaten

5 tbsp peanut oil

Chinese tomato sauce

2 tbsp butter

2 tbsp peanut oil

2 scallions, finely chopped, plus extra to garnish

2 garlic cloves, finely chopped

1-inch/2.5-cm piece fresh ginger, finely chopped

1 lb 2 oz/500 g plum tomatoes, peeled, cored, and chopped

2 tbsp tomato paste

brown sugar, to taste

3 tbsp light soy sauce

2 tsp cornstarch

5 tbsp fish stock

2 tbsp Chinese rice wine or dry sherry

93

Baked Sole with Tomato & Anchovy Sauce

1. First, make the sauce. Melt the butter with the oil in a pan. Add the onions and celery and cook over low heat, stirring occasionally, for 5 minutes, until softened. Stir in the tomatoes, tomato paste, sugar to taste, anchovy essence, marjoram, and water and season to taste with salt and pepper. Increase the heat to medium and bring to a boil, then reduce the heat and simmer, stirring occasionally, for 15–20 minutes, until thickened.

2. Meanwhile, preheat the oven to 375°F/190°C. Lightly grease a large ovenproof dish with butter. Put the sole fillets into the prepared dish.

3. Pour the sauce over the fish and bake in the preheated oven for 30 minutes, until the flesh flakes easily. Sprinkle with the chives and dill pickles and serve immediately.

Serves 4

butter, for greasing
2 lb/900 g sole fillets
1 tbsp snipped fresh chives
3 dill pickles, sliced

Tomato & anchovy sauce
※ 2 tbsp butter
※ 2 tbsp olive oil
※ 2 onions, thinly sliced
※ 1 celery stalk, finely chopped
※ 14 oz/400 g canned chopped tomatoes
※ 2 tbsp tomato paste
※ brown sugar, to taste
1 tsp anchovy essence
※ ½ tsp dried marjoram
※ scant ½ cup water
※ salt and pepper

Provençal Shrimp

1. Melt 2 tablespoons of the butter with the oil in a large flameproof casserole. Add the shrimp and cook, turning frequently, for 3–4 minutes, until they have turned pink. Remove with a slotted spoon and set aside.

2. Add the onion, garlic, celery, and bell peppers to the casserole and cook over low heat, stirring occasionally, for 5 minutes, until softened. Add the mushrooms and cook, stirring frequently, for an additional 2 minutes.

3. Stir in the tomatoes, tomato paste, sugar to taste, thyme, oregano, bay leaf, and wine and season to taste with salt and pepper. Increase the heat to medium and bring to a boil, then reduce the heat, cover, and simmer, stirring occasionally, for 15 minutes.

4. Meanwhile, put the remaining butter and the flour on a saucer and work together with your fingertips until a smooth paste (beurre manié) forms. Shape into several small balls. Add the beurre manié to the sauce, 1 piece at a time, stirring constantly. Make sure each piece has been fully incorporated before adding the next. Cook, stirring constantly, for 2–3 minutes. Return the shrimp to the casserole and simmer, stirring occasionally, for 5 minutes. Remove and discard the bay leaf. Garnish with thyme and serve immediately.

Serves 6

* 3 tbsp butter
* 2 tbsp olive oil
  2 lb 4 oz/1 kg large shrimp, peeled and deveined
* 1 small onion, finely chopped
* 3 garlic cloves, finely chopped
* 1 celery stalk, finely chopped
  1 red bell pepper and 1 yellow bell pepper, seeded and chopped
  3 cups chopped mushrooms
* 1 lb 2 oz/500 g plum tomatoes, peeled, cored, and chopped
* 2 tbsp tomato paste
* brown sugar, to taste
* 1 tbsp chopped fresh thyme, plus extra to garnish
* ½ tsp dried oregano
* 1 bay leaf
  ⅔ cup dry white wine
  2 tbsp all-purpose flour
* salt and pepper

Mussels Baked in Tomato & Basil Sauce

1. Scrub the mussels under cold running water and pull off the beards. Discard any with broken shells and any that refuse to close when tapped. Put the lemon slices in a heavy pan, add the mussels, and pour in the wine. Cover and cook over high heat, shaking the pan occasionally, for 4–6 minutes, until the shells have opened. Remove with a slotted spoon and discard any mussels that remain closed. Strain the cooking liquid through a cheesecloth-lined strainer into a bowl and set aside.

2. To make the sauce, melt the butter with the oil in a pan. Add the shallots, garlic, and celery and cook over low heat, stirring occasionally, for 5 minutes, until softened. Stir in the tomatoes, tomato paste, sugar to taste, basil, bay leaf, and the reserved cooking liquid and season to taste with salt and pepper. Increase the heat to medium and bring to a boil, then reduce the heat and simmer, stirring occasionally, for 15 minutes.

3. Meanwhile, preheat the oven to 350°F/180°C. Grease an ovenproof dish with butter. Remove the mussels from their shells. Combine the breadcrumbs and Parmesan in a bowl.

4. Remove and discard the bay leaf from the sauce and gently stir in the mussels. Pour the mixture into the prepared dish, sprinkle with the breadcrumb mixture, and bake in the preheated oven for 20 minutes, until the topping is golden and bubbling. Serve immediately.

Serves 4

4 lb 8 oz/2 kg mussels
1 lemon, sliced
⅔ cup dry white wine
butter, for greasing
2 tbsp fresh breadcrumbs
⅔ cup grated Parmesan cheese

Tomato & basil sauce
* 2 tbsp butter
* 2 tbsp olive oil
* 4 shallots, finely chopped
* 3 garlic cloves, finely chopped
* 2 celery stalks, finely chopped
* 1 lb 5 oz/600 g canned chopped tomatoes
* 2 tbsp tomato paste
* brown sugar, to taste
* 3 tbsp chopped fresh basil
* 1 bay leaf
* salt and pepper

Scallops in Tomato Sauce

1. First, make the sauce. Melt the butter with the oil in a pan. Add the shallots and garlic clove and cook over low heat, stirring occasionally, for 5 minutes, until softened. Stir in the tomatoes, tomato paste, sugar to taste, dill, parsley, mint, and water and season to taste with salt and pepper. Increase the heat to medium and bring to a boil, then reduce the heat and simmer, stirring occasionally, for 15–20 minutes, until thickened.

2. Heat the oil with the sea salt in a nonstick or heavy skillet. Add the scallops and cook for 2 minutes on each side, until golden. Remove from the pan and transfer to a serving dish.

3. Remove and discard the garlic from the sauce and spoon the sauce over the scallops. Garnish with dill and serve immediately.

Serves 4–6

2 tbsp olive oil
1 tbsp sea salt
24 scallops, shelled

Tomato sauce
* 2 tbsp butter
* 2 tbsp olive oil
2 shallots, finely chopped
* 1 garlic clove, peeled but not chopped
* 1 lb 2 oz/500 g plum tomatoes, peeled, cored, and chopped
* 2 tbsp tomato paste
* brown sugar, to taste
* 2 tbsp chopped fresh dill, plus extra to garnish
* 2 tbsp chopped fresh parsley
* 1 tbsp chopped fresh mint
* scant ½ cup water
* salt and pepper

Portuguese Eggs in Tomato Shells

① Cut a circle out of the stem end of each tomato to make an opening large enough for an egg. Using a teaspoon, carefully scoop out the seeds and pulp, without piercing the shells, and reserve. Season the insides with salt and pepper to taste. Chop the cutout circles.

② Melt the butter with the oil in a pan. Add the onion, garlic, and celery and cook over low heat, stirring occasionally, for 5 minutes, until softened. Stir in the reserved tomato seeds, pulp, and chopped circles, the tomato paste, sugar to taste, basil, and water and season to taste with salt and pepper. Increase the heat to medium and bring to a boil, then reduce the heat and simmer, stirring occasionally, for 15–20 minutes, until thickened. Remove from the heat and let cool.

③ Stand the tomato shells on a serving dish. Shell the eggs and put 1 egg into each tomato shell. Chill in the refrigerator for at least 30 minutes. Stir the mayonnaise into the cooled sauce, then transfer to a bowl, cover with plastic wrap, and chill in the refrigerator. To serve, spoon the sauce over the eggs and garnish with watercress and arugula.

Serves 6

6 large tomatoes, peeled
* 2 tbsp butter
* 2 tbsp olive oil
* 1 small onion, finely chopped
* 1 garlic clove, finely chopped
* 1 celery stalk, finely chopped
* 1 tbsp tomato paste
* brown sugar, to taste
* 1 tbsp chopped fresh basil
* 4 tbsp water
6 hard-cooked eggs
4 tbsp mayonnaise
* salt and pepper
watercress and arugula leaves, to garnish

98

Slow-Cooked Potato Stew

① Parboil the potatoes in a pan of salted boiling water for 5 minutes. Drain and set aside.

② Melt the butter with the oil in a pan. Add the bacon, onion, garlic, and celery and cook over low heat, stirring occasionally, for 5 minutes, until softened. Stir in the tomatoes, tomato paste, sugar to taste, marjoram, and stock and season to taste with salt and pepper. Increase the heat to medium and bring to a boil. Gently stir in the potatoes, reduce the heat to very low, cover, and simmer, stirring occasionally, for 45–50 minutes, until the potatoes are tender and the sauce has thickened. (Use a fork to stir gently to avoid breaking up the potatoes.)

③ Taste and adjust the seasoning, adding salt and pepper if needed. Transfer the mixture to a warmed serving dish and serve immediately.

Serves 4

1 lb 9 oz/700 g waxy potatoes, cut into 1-inch/2.5-cm cubes

✳ 2 tbsp butter

✳ 2 tbsp olive oil

2 slices bacon, chopped

✳ 1 onion, finely chopped

✳ 1 garlic clove, finely chopped

✳ 1 celery stalk, finely chopped

✳ 14 oz/400 g canned chopped tomatoes

✳ 2 tbsp tomato paste

✳ brown sugar, to taste

✳ 1 tbsp chopped fresh marjoram

scant ½ cup vegetable stock

✳ salt and pepper

Polenta, Cheese & Tomato Sauce Gratin

① Line an 11 x 7-inch/28 x 18-cm cake pan with plastic wrap. Pour the 4 cups of water into a large pan and bring to a boil. Stir the salt into the water. While stirring constantly, pour the polenta into the pan in a steady stream, then cook, stirring constantly, for 5 minutes. Stir in the mace and paprika, then pour the mixture into the prepared pan. Smooth the surface with a dampened spatula and let cool.

② To make the sauce, melt the butter with the oil in a pan. Add the onion, garlic, and celery and cook over low heat, stirring occasionally, for 5 minutes, until softened. Stir in the tomatoes, tomato paste, sugar to taste, parsley, and water and season to taste with salt and pepper. Increase the heat to medium and bring to a boil, then reduce the heat and simmer, stirring occasionally, for 15–20 minutes, until thickened.

③ Meanwhile, preheat the oven to 400°F/200°C. Grease an ovenproof dish with butter.

④ Turn out the polenta onto a cutting board and cut into 1-inch/2.5-cm squares. Remove the sauce from the heat. Put half the polenta squares into the prepared dish and spoon half the sauce over them, then sprinkle with half the cheese. Repeat the layers. Bake in the preheated oven for 30 minutes, until the topping is golden brown and bubbling. Serve immediately.

Serves 4

4 cups water

1 tsp salt

scant 2 cups instant polenta or fine cornmeal

pinch of ground mace

1 tsp paprika

butter, for greasing

¾ cup grated Gruyère or Emmental cheese

Tomato sauce

※ 2 tbsp butter

※ 2 tbsp olive oil

1 Bermuda onion, finely chopped

※ 2 garlic cloves, finely chopped

※ 1 celery stalk, finely chopped

※ 1 lb 12 oz/800 g canned chopped tomatoes

※ 2 tbsp tomato paste

※ brown sugar, to taste

※ 1 tbsp chopped fresh flat-leaf parsley

※ scant ½ cup water

※ salt and pepper

Eggplant & Potato Casserole with Tomato Sauce

1. Heat 2 tablespoons of the oil in a large skillet. Add one-third of the eggplant slices and cook over medium heat, turning occasionally, for 8–10 minutes, until evenly golden brown. Remove with a slotted spoon and drain on paper towels. Cook the remaining eggplant slices in the same way, using 4 tablespoons of the remaining oil.

2. Add the remaining oil to the skillet and heat. Add the potato slices and cook over medium heat, turning frequently, for 10 minutes, until evenly golden brown. Remove from the skillet.

3. Meanwhile, preheat the oven to 350°F/180°C. Grease an ovenproof dish with butter. Combine the thyme, pepper, and salt in a saucer. Make alternating layers of eggplant and potato slices in the prepared dish and sprinkle with the thyme mixture. Beat together the cream, eggs, and nutmeg in a bowl until thoroughly combined, then pour the mixture over the dish. Bake in the preheated oven for 45 minutes, until set.

4. Meanwhile, pour the tomato sauce into a large saucepan and place over a low heat. Heat gently until warmed through.

5. Remove the sauce from the heat and strain into a pitcher. Remove the dish from the oven, pour the sauce over it, and sprinkle with the chives. Serve immediately.

Serves 4

½ cup olive oil
3 small eggplants, thinly sliced
4 potatoes, thinly sliced
butter, for greasing
½ tsp dried thyme
½ tsp pepper
¾ tsp salt
1¼ cups light cream
5 eggs
pinch of grated nutmeg
1 quantity Basic Tomato Sauce (see page 10)
2 tbsp snipped fresh chives